DISCOVER YOUR HIDDEN PAST

Astrology reveals the past as well as the future—even past lives. Your birth chart is the key to understanding how your past lives influence your present, and how you can use this knowledge to create a better future.

Symbols of the Soul shows you how to understand the lessons of your life in the context of your spiritual evolution over many lives. The psychology of your personality and relationships is revealed as the vehicle of your soul's purpose, and the driving force of your spirit's journey.

See how the planets, signs, houses, and aspects in your chart indicate how you—a spiritual being—can best manifest your talents and destiny in this lifetime.

ABOUT THE AUTHOR

Gina Lake has a masters degree in counseling psychology. Since 1984, she has used her understanding of psychology, metaphysics, and astrology to help people understand themselves, their spiritual lessons, and their life purpose in a private counseling practice. She uses these tools to empower, encourage, and inspire her clients. She is the author of several metaphysical books, and over the past fifteen years has taught extensively in the United States and Japan. Gina can be contacted for information about her consultations by email: ginalake@msn.com.

TO WRITE TO THE AUTHOR

If you wish to contact the author or would like more information about this book, please write to the author in care of Llewellyn Worldwide and we will forward your request. Both the author and publisher appreciate hearing from you and learning of your enjoyment of this book and how it has helped you. Llewellyn Worldwide cannot guarantee that every letter written to the author can be answered, but all will be forwarded. Please write to:

Gina Lake
℅ Llewellyn Worldwide
P. O. Box 64383, Dept. K407–3
St. Paul, MN 55164-0383, U.S.A.

Please enclose a self-addressed stamped envelope for reply,
or $1.00 to cover costs. If outside U.S.A., enclose
international postal reply coupon.

GINA LAKE

SYMBOLS OF THE SOUL

DISCOVERING YOUR KARMA THROUGH ASTROLOGY

2000
Llewellyn Publications
St. Paul, Minnesota 55164-0383, U.S.A.

FIRST EDITION
First Printing, 2000

Editing and layout by Deb Gruebele
Cover design by William Merlin Cannon
Book design and project management by Eila Savela

All horoscope charts in this book were generated using WinStar © Matrix Software.

Library of Congress Cataloging-in-Publication Data
Lake, Gina, 1951 –
    Symbols of the soul : discovering your karma through astrology / Gina Lake.— 1st ed.
      p. cm.
    Includes bibliographical references.
    ISBN 1–56718–407–3
    1.Astrology. 2.Karma. I. Title.
BF1711.L35 2000
133.5—dc21

                                            99–058551
                                                CIP

Llewellyn Publications
A Division of Llewellyn Worldwide, Ltd.
P.O. Box 64383, Dept. K407–3
St. Paul, MN 55164-0383, U.S.A.
www.llewellyn.com

Printed in the United States of America

OTHER BOOKS BY GINA LAKE

A Guide to Channeling and Channeled Material

Pathways to Self Discovery: Tools to Help You Access Your Higher Self for Guidance and Healing

The Extraterrestrial Vision: The ET Agendas Past, Present, and Future

Waking Up: A Guide to Spiritual Transformation for Our Planet and Ourselves

ET Contact: Blueprint for a New World

CONTENTS

PREFACE

Some of the information in this book was obtained by nonordinary means. By that I mean that the approach presented in this book was received intuitively; but more than that, much of the information about the chart's relationship to past lives was obtained from channeling. Today this method of acquiring information is not nearly as mysterious or as suspect as even a few years ago, though it is still not routinely accepted. In fact, I would not be surprised if much of what we know about astrology came from supernatural sources when humanity was in its infancy. This cannot be proven, of course, but information from intuitives has often contributed to our knowledge and understanding.

Today astrology is being rapidly transformed. It is being elevated from its former fortunetelling status to the psycho-spiritual tool it was meant to be. This is occurring through the infusion of new information, particularly through the intuition of astrologers and the diligent attention of many psychologists. Much of what is presented in these pages is new. It is up to you to evaluate these ideas, which have proven to me the profundity of astrology. I welcome hearing about your discoveries, for that is how the body of astrological knowledge will evolve with the times.

Gina Lake, Spring 1998

INTRODUCTION

Astrology has reemerged after long being misused, misunderstood, and maligned. It is returning full force in this New Age, to be applied at last as it was meant to be—as a tool for understanding the soul's path and the personality, the soul's vehicle. Using astrology as a fortunetelling device is no longer acceptable if we are to face our lives responsibly. It is unacceptable to sit back assured that something will go our way because astrology says so. Nor is it acceptable to shrink back in fear, feeling hopeless in the face of fate. Both stances distance us from living in the moment. We must be willing to live fully in the present with confidence in the unfolding of our lives and free from the ego's need to be in control of the future.

Modern astrology, the astrology of the New Age, provides a perspective that helps us do that. It is both informative and philosophical. It informs us of our psychological needs and issues, our spiritual lessons, and our gifts, while supplying a framework within which to understand life. It demonstrates that we are connected to a Greater Whole—that we do not function separately but that we do function uniquely. It demonstrates that life is meaningful, while explaining the meaning of each life. Astrology's symbols are the soul's language of life. They reveal not only the mysteries of the universe but also the mysteries of each of our lives. In studying them, we glimpse the marvel of the universe and our role in it. They are deep and fathomless resources for psycho-spiritual insight, revealing our soul's agenda for this lifetime and the

the personality chosen to carry it out. The psyche (which means "soul") cannot be understood separate from the soul because they are related: the personality is the vehicle through which the soul accomplishes its goals. Consequently, any complete approach to astrology must therefore be a psycho-spiritual one.

What is presented here is just that—an approach that acknowledges that the life we live today is influenced and shaped by other lifetimes and other charts. We are more than our chart! We are spiritual beings and the sum total of all our earthly experiences and all our previous charts. The chart helps us understand who we are today, but it also gives us a glimpse of who we have been and where we are going. It is part of a larger journey—an evolutionary journey. Bon voyage!

NOTE

I apologize for not always finding a way to avoid the pronoun "he" when I meant "he or she." I am not comfortable using this pronoun alone, but sometimes it was too cumbersome to refer to both genders.

CHAPTER 1

THE SOUL'S PLAN

Astrology has long been used by humankind to understand himself and the universe. Early Man gazed up at the star-studded heavens and asked *why*. Is it so surprising that he also looked to the heavens for the answer? It seems that this is what he did, and astrology supplied the answers to both deep and practical questions.

Early Man felt a connection between himself and the life all around him. He saw himself as part of a Greater Whole in which he played a part, although insignificant. As Man's intellect grew, so did his sense of importance and separateness. He fell into competition with the life forms around him and sought to control them to suit his needs. Man lost his sense of interdependence with life, and astrology became just another tool for trying to control life; however, astrology, which had once represented holism, can represent it again.

We need to return to the sense of wholeness we once had. To do this, we will have to reintegrate the lost part of ourselves that provided this sense of wholeness and harmony: our spiritual Self. In fact, if we don't do this, the human race may not survive. Our current direction is destroying our most basic resources and the earth itself. If we continue, there will be little left. Maybe this is what it will take before we realize that we can survive only by working together.

What role can astrology play in this? First, it can provide the philosophical and spiritual underpinnings that are missing. Second, it can provide guidance about how to fulfill our soul's Plan, our chosen path for this lifetime. Fulfilling our Plan is important to the Whole. First, let's examine these philosophical and spiritual underpinnings. In later chapters, we will examine the chart as a means of providing individual guidance.

Astrology reveals the cyclical nature of life. It demonstrates that we are part of an orderly universe: the Moon circles around the earth, the earth circles around the Sun, one season follows another. Our lives imitate these cycles, being a microcosm of the great macrocosm. We can hardly notice these patterns and cycles without also conceding to the existence of a Higher Order, an organizing, if not creative, force—a Logos.

Astrology also suggests that life continues beyond death. What meaning would the chart have if it were not part of a larger process of evolution? What meaning would our lives have if they were not part of a larger process of evolution? Reincarnation explains many of the mysteries of life: why people are different, why suffering exists, and why some people suffer more than others. Reincarnation also explains many things about the chart that cannot be explained otherwise: some signs in our charts are more developed than other signs, and some patterns run deeper than just one lifetime could explain.

Astrology also offers us a glimpse of the perfection and wonder of the universe. For anyone who has used astrology for many years, it is its own proof of the existence of something higher. It verifies the unseen like nothing else, providing a bridge designed of symbols between the spiritual realm and the earthly one. Astrology is the esoteric translated into symbols.

Astrology also teaches us of holism, that all of life is interrelated and interdependent. In a holistic universe, the parts synergistically combine to form a whole. The whole is more than the sum of the parts, and each part is indispensable to the whole. So it is with our charts. At the same time, the whole is reflected in each of the parts: "As above, so below." The individual entering life reflects the energies present in the universe at the moment of birth. The energies of that moment can be read in the sky and are represented in the chart. Thus, the chart is a picture of the energies of that moment, which the individual born at that moment personifies.

These energies are like a costume donned for one lifetime to experience the lessons and develop the talents of those energies. Still, we are more than these energies; we are more than our charts. We are the sum total of all our previous lifetimes of experiences and their energy patterns (charts). In many ways, we are like actors on a stage: we know that we are more than the character we are playing, but for the time being we dress up in our costume and play our part. The difference is that the actor has no freedom to choose his lines and actions, and we do. This is an important difference. While the actor lives the script written for him, we create the play as we go along. We have no script. Our future, our story, is created by our choices. But is that all? Is it all choice? Let's explore this further.

Just how much of our life is predetermined and how much is created by our choices? Many of us believe that some events in life are predestined, such as certain meetings. Nevertheless, although some events may well be prearranged, how and when they take place can't be. This is determined by the circumstances and events that we create by our choices. Free will and predestination interweave in our lives. The few events in our lives that are predestined are woven into the fabric of life created by our choices and by the choices of those close to us. If you stop a moment to think about the many possible choices you and others could make, you can conclude only that the specifics of the future are not predetermined. The lessons that our soul sets out to teach us must therefore be worked into the framework already created by our choices. The soul has to "play it by ear" and wait for suitable opportunities to deliver its lessons. As a result, predicting the future is precarious, to say the least. Therefore, the Plan described in the chart can only be very general. More will be said about reading the Plan in the chapters that follow.

CHOOSING THE CHART

The soul is the vehicle of the Higher Self, that part of us that we know as God. Under the Higher Self's direction, the soul arranges and delivers our lessons. It does this by choosing a chart (choosing a moment of birth) and by arranging events. The soul reenters life when the energies provide the necessary lessons. A soul may have to wait decades before the energies it needs to attain its goals are available. However, sometimes the soul might have to be born at a particular time and place when the energies (signs) aren't quite right in order to take advantage of certain opportunities (e.g., to reunite with someone who is important to the life task or the balancing of a karmic debt, or to become part of a particular family). When that is the case, reentry can be planned so that the chart reflects the energies that are needed in other ways.

One way is to reenter life with an Ascendant that would put the Sun or several other planets in the house ruled by the desired sign. For example, if Piscean lessons are needed and no planets are in Pisces at the time needed to reenter life, the soul could arrange to reenter with an Ascendant that would put the Sun or several other planets in the twelfth house (ruled by Pisces). Reentering with a Pisces Ascendant or with the Sun conjunct Neptune (the ruler of Pisces) would also add Piscean energy. Another possibility would be to reenter when the ruler of the sign that is needed is conjunct one of the angles, which would magnify its importance in the chart.

Once we are reborn, the soul must present its lessons within the context that we have created by our choices. It cannot follow an exact plan because the context is always changing with every choice we and others make. Consequently, the soul's Plan must unfold as our life unfolds, and the specifics of how our lessons are delivered are left up to the moment of delivery. Nevertheless, some things are predictable, at least at certain points in the Plan's unfolding, because once a set of circumstances is set in motion, it often plays itself out predictably. Let's look at some examples, which show how the soul works in our lives.

Suppose someone needs to learn patience. Besides choosing Aries or Taurus as a theme in the chart (both signs teach patience), the soul might arrange for that person to meet someone whose Mars falls on his Uranus. This person is likely to stimulate the Uranus individual's need for change and excitement, and provoke impulsive and dangerous acts. This could teach the Uranus individual to be more patient by causing him to confront the negative consequences of his impatience. Patience can be taught many ways. The point is that the soul's involvement reaches beyond choosing a chart to ongoing participation in creating whatever lessons are needed.

Here is another example, this time about a mother and her son. In a previous lifetime, the mother was the son, and the son was the mother, an exact reversal of current roles. In the past, the mother had harmed her son by neglecting him. Currently, the mother, who was the son previously, will have the choice of either caring or not caring for her son. If she doesn't care for him, the karma would not be balanced and her own growth would be marred because two wrongs truly do not make a right. She is likely to care for her child rather than neglect him, however, because of the compassion she gained from her own experience of being neglected. How, then, is the child to learn his lesson? Through love. Although it may seem that most learning comes from pain, this is not always true. In this instance, the son, who had neglected his son in the past, will learn to care for others by being cared for. We learn to love by experiencing love.

The astrological chart's role in this is simple: the chart represents the personality (or energy pattern) chosen to bring about the lessons. More specifically, the personality is chosen to help balance a karmic debt, to learn basic life lessons, and to complete a life task. More will be said about the last two objectives in later chapters. For now, let's concentrate on understanding how the chart in our example was chosen to help balance the karmic debt.

The son's soul selected a chart that would help him learn compassion and repay the debt owed the mother from harm inflicted on her in the past. To develop his compassion and desire to serve, his chart had a strong Pisces theme. To create feelings of loyalty and responsibility toward her, he reentered life when the Moon was conjunct her Saturn.

Out of nearly infinite possibilities, the soul must find a chart to fit the karmic lessons, the basic lessons, and the life task. However, the lessons, particularly the karmic lessons, are the first priority in choosing a chart. In our earlier lifetimes, this job is simplified because our lessons and our life task are usually one and the same. In these lifetimes, we are busy learning the basic lessons of life. In our later lifetimes, when the lessons and the life task are different, the life task is usually chosen to fit with the lessons. This is helpful to keep in mind when trying to identify the lessons and the life task in the chart. One way a more specific lesson or life task can be facilitated is through a chart with a strong theme, since it will not lend itself as easily to divergent paths. People who have charts with strong themes find themselves following a narrower course, allowing for greater opportunity to encounter certain people or experiences needed for their growth.

The Higher Self guides us through intuition. It speaks to us intuitively about our Plan and what we need to learn. We may or may not listen, but we all can intuit these messages to some extent. Our Higher Selves also can communicate with each other and often do when enlisting each other's help in our Plans, but because people do not always listen to their Higher Self, and because people's choices are unpredictable, each Plan is both general and flexible.

KARMA

Karma is often thought of as "an eye for an eye and a tooth for a tooth." This is simplistic and doesn't take into account the complex processes involved in human growth and evolution. "As you sow, so shall you reap" encompasses the meaning of karma better, but this also doesn't do justice to the complexity of this law.

There are two misunderstandings that contribute to the confusion about karma: that we are born bad and that we must be punished for our sins. Both beliefs are related to the Garden of Eden myth, which forms the basis of Judeo-Christian thought. The concept that God punishes us is a childish conception of God. Karma is a natural law of the universe and a tool for the evolution of humankind. It is governed by love, as is all of life, and it cannot be born of retribution and punishment. To equate karma with punishment is to underestimate the Creator's wisdom and love.

A distinction should be made between lessons and karmic debts. We all have lessons that are part of our evolution. Karmic debts, on the other hand, originate from choices that caused serious injury or death. Because karmic debts often cannot be balanced in one lifetime, they must be arranged for in the soul's Plan and not just introduced when an opportunity arises, as with many other lessons. A karmic debt may well be the overriding consideration in determining when the soul will reenter life and what astrological energies will be taken on. If a karmic debt is to be balanced in a particular lifetime, that will shape the chart, and the other lessons and the life task will be secondary to it. If a debt is significant enough, it may even be the life task. Whenever a significant debt is to be balanced, it will be apparent in the chart, although lesser ones may not.

Any act resulting in serious injury or death must be balanced. This is not necessarily done by experiencing the same act, but by learning whatever is necessary to prevent it from happening again and by making amends to the victim. The term "karmic debt" is at the root of some of our misconceptions about karma and how it works, since "debt" implies punishment or retribution. "Lesson" would be more fitting, since balancing a karmic debt involves learning as well as making amends to the victim. It is true that a lesson is often taught by putting the offender in the victim's shoes to instill the empathy and understanding needed to prevent a similar tragedy from recurring. Although role-reversal is a common way karmic debts are balanced, this doesn't mean that the perpetrator becomes the victim at the hands of his or her former victim, or that the function of a role-reversal is punitive. What follows are some stories that illustrate how karma works.

In a former lifetime, Celeste was abused by her father, who is now her husband. People often choose to reincarnate together to continue their relationship—even an abusive one. It would not be surprising under these circumstances if the pattern of abuse established earlier was to continue. This often happens until the one who is abused recognizes that it is detrimental. The abuse continued until Celeste realized that she deserved more. She had to come to this realization before the balancing could take place. The soul often allows us to learn as much from our choices as possible, intervening to establish karmic repayment only after we realize a debt is owed. Once the realization has dawned, the balancing can begin immediately if circumstances allow it.

Celeste pressed charges against her husband who, as a result, was incarcerated for assault and received counseling. He was also required to pay monetary damages, which helped her start a new life. However, just because the husband served time and paid damages does not ensure the debt's release. This depends on the changes in the perpetrator's understanding. For one person a certain sentence might be more than enough, while for another, five times that might not be enough. Needless to say, the criminal justice system often does a poor job of teaching and sometimes does more harm than good. Nevertheless, it is society's way of trying to carry out the soul's work, and it often does. In this case, the punishment did not teach the lesson. So the soul will have to find other ways to further the perpetrator's understanding, which may or may not involve the victim. The karmic debt is not always balanced under circumstances that include the victim, but frequently the victim also has something to gain from further interaction with the perpetrator. In that case, the two may meet again.

Another woman, Denise, left her husband. The marriage had been necessary to complete a debt lingering from a previous lifetime. Once the debt was balanced, Denise was free to move on. Many other lifetimes had been spent with her former husband to balance the karma incurred when he killed her. He was required to take care of her during these lifetimes to gain the understanding he needed. By caring for her as an invalid, as his dying mother, as a sick child, and as a wounded soldier, he gained respect for the preciousness of life, which was his lesson. Releasing karma is not as simple as many might think. It is never known if the pre-arranged circumstances will serve the intended purpose. Circumstances are arranged by the soul before life, but what is done with those circumstances is up to those involved. Sometimes a situation intended to balance karma fails. When that happens, the individuals usually disengage and try again another time.

Some think having karma with someone means staying with him or her no matter what. However, karma does not require us to stay in unhappy or unhealthy relationships. Unhappiness is often a sign that a soul's needs are not being met, and sometimes the relationship must dissolve before those needs can be met. This is not to deny the value of commitment, but some people use their belief in karma as an excuse for not risking change. In a karmic relationship, when no further release of karma can take place under the circumstances created by the couple, it may be best for them to separate and continue on alone. Their Plans may need to be adjusted if the karmic balancing was an important element of their Plans, but that can usually be arranged.

Sometimes couples, whose initial purpose for being together was karmic, decide to remain together to develop their love more fully even after the karma is balanced. Many of our most meaningful and long-lasting relationships begin this way. Having shared lessons with someone creates a bond that often lasts beyond the dissolution of karma.

Tana experienced a painful death in a former lifetime at the hands of someone who broke into her home and robbed and killed her. This experience was reflected in fearful behavior, especially in her fear of being alone. She didn't have to meet her killer again in this lifetime, but her fear needed to be balanced, and her killer needed to balance this incident for his own soul's growth. Whenever someone is seriously harmed, not only will the perpetrator need to learn something and make amends to the victim, but the victim will invariably need to heal and readjust his or her outlook as well. The souls of those involved must find ways to accomplish this, whether through meeting again or through separate experiences.

Tana's soul sought to balance her fear and build her confidence by arranging circumstances in which she could be a heroine. When an earthquake shook her small village, she experienced an inner strength and calm that she didn't know she had. She used it to lead others and herself to safety before another quake completely destroyed the area. By arranging for her safety during the earthquake and by projecting her True Self to her then, her soul helped her experience the courage of her Being, which left a positive imprint on her psyche.

For the man who had harmed her in a former lifetime, the story was different. He needed to learn what it means to have to earn a living. In his next life, he was placed in circumstances in which he would have to work hard to provide for himself. To make it less likely that he would choose robbery again when faced with hard work, religious parents who would set an example of honest labor and accomplishment were selected.

The last story is about a man who is trying to overcome a phobia of horses. A rampaging wild horse killed him in a lifetime during the taming of the West. He died in this manner to balance his young daughter's death, which happened when he allowed her to go unsupervised into a pen of horses. On the surface, this looks like "an eye for an eye," but it proved to be just the experience he needed to teach him about the fragility of human life. If he had appreciated this then, he would not have let his young child wander unsupervised. Her death impressed her with the fragility of life. One would expect the father to have learned this, too, but because he saw his daughter's death as her fault rather than his, he needed to learn it some other way. His soul chose the trampling to teach the lesson. Although this may seem harsh, death is a natural part of life and has many teachings for us. We all die traumatically many, many times during our evolution. Traumatic death is a way of teaching something dramatically. From the soul's perspective, death is merely a stage in the eternity of life and another means of teaching life's lessons.

READING THE KARMIC DEBT IN THE CHART

A karmic debt, or repayment for one, will be indicated in a chart if balancing the debt will shape that lifetime; but because being owed a debt is indicated in the chart by the same factors as owing one, we cannot tell from the chart alone which situation is being described. Furthermore, since many lifetimes may be needed to balance a karmic debt, the same debt may show up over many lifetimes in the charts of those involved. Since each lifetime is likely to pay off a little more of the debt, any debt indicated in a chart will be somewhere in this process of release. Unfortunately, we cannot tell the extent of the debt remaining from the chart alone. Nevertheless, if a debt is reflected in the chart, it will shape that life somehow. For example, if a small portion of a debt between two individuals remains, the souls may arrange to meet and marry to release it once and for all. Even though the debt is small, the marriage would structure and define both their lives until the debt is balanced.

What form the repayment will take depends on several things. The one who has incurred a debt is given opportunities to repay it according to his or her abilities and the needs of the one owed. The debt may be repaid through aid of some sort, monetary or material compensation, or some other means depending on the needs of the one who is owed for that particular lifetime. Obviously, if the one who is owed is already wealthy, monetary compensation may not be of sufficient value to balance the debt unless the debt is slight.

If a karmic debt or repayment is indicated, it is likely to be symbolized by challenging Saturn aspects or by several planets in the twelfth house. The aspects most likely to indicate this are Saturn squares and oppositions to the Sun or the Moon. Saturn squares or oppositions to Venus or Mars also may indicate a debt, but one that will have a lesser impact on shaping that lifetime. Although these aspects are not the only indicators of a debt, this is the only generalization that can be made. The absence of these aspects does not necessarily mean that no karmic debt exists, however. Their presence just makes it likely that a karmic debt will shape that particular lifetime.

A karmic debt or repayment is likely if one or more planets are found in the twelfth house, especially if they are the Sun, the Moon, Venus, Mars, Saturn, Neptune, or Pluto. If several planets are in this house, the karmic debt or repayment is likely to play a significant role in that lifetime. The planets in the twelfth house and aspects to them, the sign on the twelfth house cusp and its ruler, any other sign in the twelfth house and its ruler, the ruler's house, and aspects to the ruler provide information about karma. Taken together, these chart factors describe the circumstances in a past life or lifetimes under which the karma was created. Saturn's house, sign, and aspects describe how this karma might be met. Although there is no guarantee that the debt will be paid, the opportunity to repay it will be through the sign and house placement of Saturn, and signs and houses related to Saturn by aspect. The following example illustrates how a karmic debt can be read in a chart.

In the first chart, the chart of a woman, Saturn is in Virgo in the ninth house opposite the Sun in Pisces in the third house and square the Moon in Gemini in the seventh house. The twelfth house is empty with Scorpio on its cusp and its ruler in Leo in the eighth house. If there were planets in the twelfth house, the ruler's placement would be less significant. Given this, the karmic debt may have involved an intimate relationship in which control was an issue (Scorpio ruling the twelfth house and its ruler in Leo in Scorpio's house). It cannot be known who dominated whom until this hypothesis is checked out with the person to whom the chart belongs, who may be able to identify this relationship. In this case, the chart belongs to the one owed the debt.

Next, by looking at Saturn's placement in the ninth house in Virgo, we can form some hypotheses about how this karma might be balanced. The ninth house rules long distance travel, higher education, philosophy, and religious thought. The debtor might repay her by taking her on a trip, putting her through college, or expanding her outlook or ideas. In fact, the debtor, currently a man, either gave to her or had the opportunity to give to her in all the above ways. Saturn's sign indicates other opportunities through which the karma can be balanced. In this case, the debtor worked at menial tasks (Saturn in Virgo) to provide for her. Saturn's aspects also describe the circumstances in which the karma is likely to be balanced. In the woman's chart, Saturn is opposite her Pisces Sun and Mercury in the third house and square her Gemini Moon in the seventh house. As it happened, the man and the woman met in high school through a brother (third house) and were married (seventh house).

The man's chart provides additional information about balancing the debt. Although he does not have Saturn square or opposite his Sun or Moon, he does have Pluto conjunct his Moon and opposite his Venus, the ruler of his Descendant. Venus is in his third house, indicating the high school relationship; and the Pluto/Moon conjunction is in his ninth house, portraying the method of repayment mentioned earlier. Saturn is in Libra, which also rules his twelfth house, indicating possible karma pertaining to a relationship. Venus, the ruler of his twelfth house and his Descendant, is in Aquarius, indicating her abrupt departure in this lifetime (Uranus, the ruler of Aquarius, is known for sudden disruptions and upheavals), which caused him considerable pain (Pluto/Moon opposite Venus). So his chart is more descriptive of the situation that delivered the lesson than hers because he was more affected by it than she was.

The next example involves a man, now deceased, who was married to a woman to whom he owed a debt. The husband needed to learn something, which was possible only within the context of a relationship with the individual whom he had injured in the past, who was now his wife. At the same time, it was important that his wife receive financial remuneration from him to bolster her confidence and pride, which had been damaged by their previous encounter. The relationship was difficult for both, yet they stayed together for over thirty years. When a karmic debt exists between two people, it creates a strong bond until the debt is balanced. If a relationship is karmic and requires two people to remain together, they will either stay together without question, or circumstances will be such that separation is inconceivable. If the situation no longer allows for the debt to be balanced, either their sense of commitment will change or circumstances will change, or both.

Aries rules the man's twelfth house, and its ruler is in Capricorn in the tenth house. Saturn is widely opposite his Sun and square his Moon, which is conjunct Pluto. This configuration supports the possibility of a karmic debt. As we saw in the previous example and as we will see in the chapter on aspects, Pluto, as well as Saturn, often points to a karmic debt. With Pluto aspecting the Moon, the debt is likely to involve the wife (if the individual is a man) or the mother. With Aries ruling the twelfth house, its ruler (Mars) in Capricorn (ruled by Saturn), and Pluto involved with Saturn and the two luminaries, the event in the former lifetime probably involved violence and death. This chart describes a debt in many of its factors, making its significance in that lifetime all the more likely.

The Moon/Pluto conjunction and the Sun (both in aspect to Saturn) fall in the man's second and sixth houses respectively, indicating that the debt is likely to be paid by working hard and providing material comforts to the one to whom he owes the debt. Since this debt is apparently significant, it is not surprising that the remainder of his chart provides the energy and drive necessary to make a good livelihood. Mars in Capricorn in the tenth house provides a drive for achievement, security, and status. Taurus rising and the Moon in the second house provide a drive for material comforts and the persistence to obtain them. The Sun and Venus in the sixth house provide devotion to a medical profession. Finally, Jupiter in the fourth house ensures commitment to family.

If these examples alone are not convincing, study people in your own life. Karma cannot be interpreted easily from the chart without knowing specifics about the individual and without excellent intuition. If it can't be done skillfully, it shouldn't be attempted. This information is not presented with the expectation that you will be able to delineate the karma of every chart, but to show you how karma works and is represented in the chart. If you talk with others about the karma you see in their charts, be careful not to sound negative or preachy. The only purpose for giving karmic information to others is to increase their understanding of their lessons and their life purpose. If it doesn't serve this end, then don't reveal it. This subject must be handled very sensitively.

DELINEATING THE TWELFTH HOUSE

The following descriptions are offered to help delineate the twelfth house and any karma that may be represented there. The goal is not to uncover the specifics behind the karma, but to get a sense of what needs to be learned. Please keep in mind that these descriptions will not apply to every chart. Not everyone has a karmic debt or one that can be seen in the chart. The following interpretations assume that a karmic debt is indicated, specifically by challenging Saturn or Pluto aspects. Also keep in mind that twelfth-house factors may describe something that happened to the person rather than something for which he or she is karmically responsible. The rest of the chart will provide clues about whether the person owes a debt or is due one.

The description following each sign applies if the sign rules the twelfth house, if the sign's ruling planet is in the twelfth house, or if the ruler of the sign on the twelfth house cusp is in that sign or in that sign's natural house (e.g., the first house is Aries' natural house, the second house is Taurus', and so on). If several planets are in the twelfth house, the sign descriptions will have to be intuitively synthesized. These descriptions are only guidelines. You will also have to use your intuition, analyze the rest of the chart, and talk to the person to whom the chart belongs to arrive at an interpretation of the twelfth house.

Aries

When Aries is related to the twelfth house, the karmic debt may stem from injury or death from a violent act, often the result of unleashed anger or rage. The cause of the rage may be described by other planets or signs involved with the twelfth house. If Saturn or Capricorn are also involved, a death is likely to have occurred. Because Aries usually represents intentional rather than accidental violence, this sign can indicate some of the most difficult karma. Because karma this serious takes many lifetimes to balance, and because it may be at any stage in this process, the debt indicated may be large or small.

Violent acts require a variety of lessons, depending on the cause of the act, and a chart will be chosen accordingly. When controlling anger is the lesson, a Taurus, Virgo, or Capricorn Moon may be present; Saturn may be square or conjunct Mars; fire may be absent; the Sun or Mars may be in hard aspect to one or more of the outer planets; or earth and air will be emphasized to add distance to the feelings. The possibilities are in no way exhausted by this list.

When we are enraged, we often lose sight of the value of life and our potential for destruction. Therefore, gaining an appreciation for life's preciousness and fragility may be another lesson when Aries is related to the twelfth house. When it is, the Moon's nodes are often found in the twelfth and sixth houses, and the lesson is learned through a life task of service in the healing professions.

The proper use of one's energy and will may be another lesson with Aries related to the twelfth house. In this case, the goal would not only be controlling one's anger but also gaining awareness of one's needs so that anger would not accumulate in the first place. A chart with an emphasis in Scorpio to increase introspection would help with this lesson. An emphasis in the air signs to add objectivity would also make a healthy use of emotion more likely, as would family members who could serve as positive role models.

For someone who has acted violently in a past life, respect for life in general may be lacking, and an appreciation for the value of being alive may be needed. If this is the case, the soul's approach may be to teach the beauty and pleasure of life by providing circumstances in the next life that are pleasant, happy, and abundant. An environment that is peaceful, loving, and respectful of life is often what is needed to balance a violent act in a former lifetime. To help with this, Jupiter may be conjunct the Sun, Ascendant, or Moon, adding protectiveness and good fortune, or the chart may be favorably aspected in other ways.

Taurus

When Taurus is related to the twelfth house, stealing, giving too little, or giving too much may be responsible for a karmic debt. Greed leading to criminal acts that caused injury or death is the most serious possibility. Other possibilities are waste or frivolousness that caused suffering through deprivation, or selfishness that harmed someone, like in the story "Cinderella." Injury caused by encouraging gluttony, spoiling someone, or failing to instill proper values are still other possibilities. These last offenses may not take as long to balance as something more severe, but some sort of balancing is still likely.

When Taurus is related to the twelfth house, the lesson also may be about values. Those whose greed causes them to steal may need to learn that material things do not bring happiness, love, or fulfillment. One way the soul teaches this is by arranging for the individual to have more money than he or she can ever enjoy—coupled with loneliness. This demonstrates the emptiness of material things, especially if love is not present amidst the wealth.

Sharing is another lesson that might be in order. Although a degree of spiritual development is necessary before we are capable of selfless giving, generosity can be taught. One way this is done is through a watery chart, which increases empathy and sensitivity. Loving family members also help by modeling generosity and providing the experience of being given to. Paradoxically, we do not learn to share by being forced to as much as by being given to. When our own needs are met, we willingly give to others. Therefore, the soul will not usually use a neglectful or unloving environment to teach unselfishness, but a loving one in which all the primary needs are met.

Those who suffered from gluttony or inflicted it on others in a former lifetime may need to learn the benefits of moderation. A chart that is conservative, frugal, self-disciplined, and self-sacrificing can be used to teach this. Any combination of Capricorn, Virgo, and Pisces is likely to be helpful. However, Pisces' lack of discipline may not be helpful to some. The soul also may choose a family with these characteristics or one that is not prosperous.

Gemini

When Gemini is related to the twelfth house, misuse of the power of communication or the careless use of a vehicle may have caused someone harm in a former lifetime. Intent is important in determining the extent of the karma. Unintentional or inadvertent harm is likely to require only minimal karmic balancing. One possibility is that the individual spread injurious rumors, either true or false. If he or she was in a position of power with access to many people, the karma could be extensive. A prime example would be using the media to damage someone's reputation. If abuse of power is involved, Pluto or Scorpio is likely to be related to the twelfth house, in addition to Mercury (Gemini).

Correct use of the power of communication is taught several ways. One is by inhibiting the individual's ability to communicate, which demonstrates the power of the word. For this, Saturn may be in Gemini, in the third house, or aspecting Mercury. Another is by putting someone who abused power in an influential position. Then, if he or she abuses power again, the consequences would be great; or perhaps he or she might be on the receiving end of someone else's abuse of power.

If an injury or death resulted from the careless use of a vehicle because of a lack of responsibility, poor judgment, negligence, carelessness, or indecision, balancing will probably be necessary. However, not everyone operating a vehicle that injures someone incurs karma. If karma is incurred, what is needed to balance it depends on the cause of the accident. If greater responsibility, caution, or judgment is needed, Capricorn may be present in the chart. If greater decisiveness is needed, fixed signs may be present. The soul has ways of developing these traits, though they usually come as a matter of course with age and spiritual development.

Cancer

When Cancer is related to the twelfth house, the karma probably involved a family member. Since the family is one of the main arenas in which life's lessons are taught, karma is often incurred with family members. The family is also the most common arena for releasing a karmic debt because of the mutual dependency and closeness demanded by these relationships. When Mars or Pluto is also involved with the twelfth house, the incident is likely to have involved violence and physical harm, perhaps even sexual abuse. Otherwise, emotional abuse or neglect is likely.

If the chart is the perpetrator's, compassion and empathy are needed, and the chart will support this. To teach this, the perpetrator may experience dependency or powerlessness in some form. Retardation, disabilities, and mental illness are just a few of the more extreme conditions that lend themselves to teaching this. There also are milder ways of teaching compassion and empathy, of course. The soul will choose circumstances that fit the individual. If the chart belongs to the victim, it will support his or her healing.

Leo

When Leo is related to the twelfth house, the incident responsible for the karmic debt probably involved an abuse of the individual's influence or power, possibly for his or her own advancement. If the incident involved self-advancement at someone else's expense, a greater appreciation for the needs of others is in order. To help balance a tendency toward self-service, the chart might be oriented toward service.

Another possibility is that the individual used his or her power to control others. In this case, a respect for autonomy and freedom may be taught by an experience of being controlled. The inhumanity and immorality of controlling others becomes obvious when the tables are turned. Regardless of how it seems, this is not retribution but an efficient way of readjusting someone's attitude.

The victim who has Leo related to the twelfth house may suffer from feelings of inadequacy and a tendency to give his or her power away. This is frequently the result of having been oppressed or controlled by others. In that case, the rest of the chart will support the development of ego-strength and confidence.

Virgo

When Virgo is related to the twelfth house, enslavement or mistreatment of someone under one's service may be behind the karmic debt. Enslavement must have caused physical or psychological damage for it to require balancing, however. Not all slave owners, for instance, are karmically indebted to their slaves. The purpose of karma is to balance a wrong attitude or action. If a slave owner's intentions and treatment of his slaves were good, then little or no karmic balancing would be necessary. If not, the karmic requirement could be great.

A common way to balance this is to make the offender a slave or servant, which affords him or her the experience of this perspective.

Sometimes, however, this only reinforces the individual's disdain for servants. If that happens, several more lifetimes of servitude may be needed before the lesson is learned. Some people are susceptible to seeing themselves as superior to others no matter what their lot in life is. They are both the ones most likely to mistreat others when in a position of power and those hardest to teach this lesson to. We all have certain lessons that come harder than others.

The victim with Virgo ruling this house may suffer from low self-esteem and difficulty being the master of his or her destiny. When this is the case, the chart will be chosen carefully to teach this lesson.

Libra

When Libra is related to the twelfth house, the karmic debt is likely to have involved a marriage or other partnership. If it was a business partnership, one person's dishonesty, abusive treatment, or irresponsibility may have harmed the other. If it was a marriage, one of the partners may have been harmed because of the other's behavior. What the balancing will entail depends on the offense and why it happened.

If selfishness or greed was responsible for the injury, the rest of the chart will reflect the need to be more generous and cooperative (if the chart is the debtor's), with Libra and Pisces likely themes. Chart factors that might be chosen to teach this are: little or no fire; many oppositions; Neptune, Venus, or the Moon conjunct an angle; a Libra Sun or Libra rising; or the Sun in the seventh house. Other circumstances may also be arranged to teach this, such as being born into a large family where sharing and cooperation are necessities.

Scorpio

When Scorpio is related to the twelfth house, a karmic debt resulting from emotional or sexual abuse is possible. If the chart belongs to the perpetrator, he or she will need to learn empathy, compassion, and love. If it is the victim's, he or she will need to heal.

Another possibility when Scorpio is related to the twelfth house is past business dealings that pursued power and wealth with little or no regard for others. Large corporations that take advantage of people in impoverished countries would be an example of this, or the small businessperson who may regularly participate in graft, tax evasion, or petty theft.

One way the soul teaches empathy and compassion is through certain signs, most notably Pisces and Cancer. The soul may also arrange for the perpetrator to experience powerlessness and dependency to discourage him or her from taking advantage of others again. Although this sounds punitive, it is often the only way to teach empathy and compassion.

Sagittarius

When Sagittarius is related to the twelfth house, it may indicate a karmic debt resulting from an irresponsible or careless act. In particular, it may indicate a mistake made while traveling or exploring that resulted in injury or death. Another possibility is that Sagittarian self-centeredness may have led to neglecting the needs of others and inadvertently harming them. Since the harm caused in these instances is rarely intentional, usually the balancing simply entails learning to be more careful and responsible.

Life has a way of teaching us what we need to learn through remorse, other people, the criminal justice system, or a repetition of the incident. If greater care, common sense, and responsibility are not learned through these means, they are taught easily enough through the earth signs, aspects to Saturn, and a respite from Sagittarian lifetimes. Therefore, if a chart with Sagittarius related to the twelfth house shows signs of a karmic debt, as well as strength in earth or a strong Saturn, it is likely to have been chosen to balance irresponsibility or carelessness. On the other hand, if the chart does not support caution and responsibility, it may mean that the individual experienced the results of someone else's irresponsibility in a former lifetime. In that case, repayment may be received in that lifetime.

Capricorn

When Capricorn is related to the twelfth house, it may indicate a karmic debt involving a death. Being responsible for someone's death is a serious offense. However, whether or not it was intentional is important in determining the extent of the debt and the lesson needed to balance it. The planets in the house, the twelfth house ruler's house and sign, and aspects to these planets may describe the circumstances surrounding the death.

The subject of killing brings up the question of whether executioners, soldiers, and abortionists incur karma. Some karma is incurred in each of these instances, but these forms of killing are not on the same level as murder. Nevertheless, we incur societal karma by belonging to a society that allows these things. Of these three types of killing, abortion is the least serious because in almost every case the soul has not yet entered the body.

When someone is killed, the person responsible may need to gain an appreciation for the preciousness of human life. One way of teaching this is for the person to experience his or her own life cut short or to lose a loved one. If the death was unintentional, what is needed depends on the individual and what caused the death.

Those who were killed may benefit from fire in their charts to give them more courage and confidence. Violent or sudden deaths invariably leave the victim with a sense of vulnerability and distrust. As a result, victims' charts are not likely to have a strong Capricorn theme, which would only increase their fear. By studying the rest of the chart and using our imaginations and intuition, we can often determine whether the chart belongs to the perpetrator or the victim.

Aquarius

When Aquarius is related to the twelfth house, it may indicate a karmic debt resulting from sudden, accidental injury or death caused by impatience or a lack of judgment. Many of these kinds of mistakes never need balancing because the negative consequences teach what needs to be learned. However, some people, especially those who blame others for their mistakes, may need further lessons and a chart that encourages caution and self-restraint. In that case, the rest of the chart will bear that out. On the other hand, if the chart belongs to the victim of someone else's careless action, the rest of the chart will encourage confidence and courage rather than caution and patience.

Pisces

When Pisces is related to the twelfth house, emotional damage or neglect may be responsible for a karmic debt. With Pisces, the emotional damage is not likely to have been inflicted intentionally or violently. More likely, it resulted from not being able to provide care because of mental illness, physical disability, mental retardation, or drug or alcohol addiction.

The balancing depends on what was underlying the neglect. If it was due to drug or alcohol addiction, being born to alcoholic parents is a common remedy. This provides an opportunity for developing empathy and for facing this problem again in order to overcome it once and for all. If more ego-strength or practical abilities are needed, an earthy chart will help. However, because ego-strength is a function of soul-age, the individual may need more experience with life before being able to cope with the world. If a physical or mental handicap was responsible for the neglect, the situation is more complex. The soul analyzes each situation to determine what is needed.

Victims of neglect will have to learn to see themselves as other than victims. To accomplish this, the chart and childhood circumstances must be chosen carefully to balance feelings of unworthiness. A loving and attentive family coupled with a fiery chart and a favorably placed Jupiter for ease can do much to offset such damage.

CHAPTER 2

THE LIFE TASK AND THE LIFE LESSON

The life task and the life lesson are related and usually cannot be adequately understood without regarding them as such. It will be necessary, however, to describe separately how the life task and the life lesson are revealed in the chart. Since the Moon's nodes are key in understanding both, as well as their relationship, let's begin by looking at what they represent.

THE MOON'S NODES

The Moon's nodes convey a single message about the life task, what might be used in it, and what might interfere with it. The life task will use the characteristics of the North Node's sign and be related to the area of life designated by the North Node's house. Inhibiting factors will be characteristics represented by the

South Nodes' sign and the area of life designated by the South Node's house, as well as challenging aspects to the North Node.

The Moon's nodes are the two points where the Moon's orbit intersects the plane of the ecliptic. They are associated with emotional, nurturing relationships because of their connection with the Moon. The transits of the Moon's nodes affect our primary relationships, particularly our familial and love relationships. These transits often bring new, significant relationships into our lives or remove those that no longer serve our Plan.

Because our primary relationships are deeply tied to our lessons and to our Plan, it is not surprising that a connection exists between our lessons, our life task, and our relationships, and that the Moon's nodes represent all three. Nearly every lesson and life task includes at least one other person. Fulfillment of a karmic debt, for instance, is nearly always carried out within a relationship. The personality's basic lessons, to be covered in the next chapter, need others as foils as well. Others also help us eliminate our negative patterns by modeling new behaviors. Even lessons pertaining to being alone are accomplished by contrasting aloneness with companionship. Our life lessons and our life tasks are irrevocably intertwined with others, who act as teachers, foils, and cocreators in our drama.

CHART THEMES

The chart themes in concert with the Moon's nodes and Saturn describe both the life task and the life lesson. The themes, represented primarily by the prominent signs of the chart, reveal both our lessons and the gifts likely to be used in the life task, depending on the development of the signs representing them. Signs that have been chosen repeatedly in past lives are more developed and, as a result, more likely to be expressed positively. The more lifetimes spent with a sign, the greater the attunement to that energy and the easier it is to express it skillfully.

Our gifts are the positive characteristics of our most developed signs, while our lessons or challenges are the negative characteristics of our least developed signs. This means that if we have a concentration of planets in a highly developed sign, we will be especially gifted in the talents of that sign. These gifts will undoubtedly be used in our life task and in overcoming our challenges. On the other hand, if we have a concentration of planets in an undeveloped sign, we will be confronted repeatedly with the lessons of that sign.

How a sign is expressed depends on more than just past life experience. Stressful circumstances make it more likely that we will express the negative side of the signs in our chart, or at least the negative side of the more undeveloped ones. Age is another factor: the younger we are, the less likely we are to express our chart skillfully.

Determining which signs in a chart are problematic and which ones are not is not always easy. The main clues are found in the sign and house placements of Saturn and the South Node, and the signs on the eighth and twelfth house cusps. Each of these signs and houses represents potentially problematic psychological tendencies developed in former lifetimes. Of course, the individual can tell you how he or she is expressing the chart. However, keep in mind that someone who has not had a Saturn return (which occurs between ages twenty-eight and twenty-nine) may be expressing a sign negatively simply out of immaturity. Beyond this, intuition must be your guide.

The themes are uncovered by noting the signs of the Ascendant and the personal planets (the Sun, the Moon, Mercury, Venus, and Mars), which houses are most heavily occupied by planets, and which planets are placed on an angle (conjunct the Ascendant, Midheaven, Descendant, or Nadir) or most heavily aspected. Nearly every chart has at least one prominent theme, many have several, and only a few have no major theme but many minor ones.

THE LIFE TASK

Each of us has a task to accomplish in life. It may or may not involve our occupation, but it is often related to it. There are many different kinds of life tasks. The life task can be as simple as learning to cook and take care of oneself or as complex as discovering DNA, with no life task being more important than another. Whatever the life task, its value lies in the contribution it makes toward our evolution. Although the life task is not spelled out specifically before life, it is identifiable in a general way in the chart through the themes and the North Node.

To understand the North Node's message, we need to note its sign, its house, its ruler's sign and house, and aspects to it and its ruler, as well as the houses related by aspect to it and its ruler. Synthesizing these factors with the chart themes provides a general idea of the life task.

These factors point to the life task, but they will never reveal exactly what it is because it hasn't been created yet. Only occasionally, when the life task is a continuation of an earlier one, are the specifics laid out before life. We are not here to live out a predetermined plan but to create our lives through our choices and to learn from these choices.

Let's take, for example, the North Node in the third house. What we know about this placement is that the life task will involve learning or teaching or both. The subjects of interest to this individual will be described by the themes in the chart and the other signs and houses related to the North Node. For instance, someone with the North Node in the third house and five planets in the eighth house may study and eventually teach others about psychology, metaphysics, sex, or money management. This is especially true if one of those eighth-house planets is the ruler of the North Node's sign or related by aspect to the North Node.

THE NORTH NODE IN THE HOUSES AND SIGNS

The North Node's house and related houses describe the areas of life that will involve the life task. The North Node's sign and related signs indicate qualities that will be needed and further refined by the life task. These qualities will be exercised while pursuing the life task and, therefore, further developed. Nevertheless, to some extent, the house and sign placements are interchangeable (e.g., the North Node in the first house is similar to the North Node in Aries, the North Node in the second house is similar to the North Node in Taurus, and so on). Keep this in mind in delineating the nodes.

The North Node in the First House or in Aries

This placement of the North Node indicates the importance of initiative and independent action to the life task. Those with this placement must develop their independence, initiative, individualism, and leadership skills to fulfill their life task. The life task often requires courage and individual initiative and might involve pioneering or discovery. Developing themselves and creating a strong identity are important to balance dependency in former lifetimes. They need to learn to follow their impulses and drives, and be the master of their own destiny. They need the freedom to pursue their natural inclinations. If initiative and self-development are not undertaken, and dependence on others persists, they will find themselves in situations demanding greater independence and initiative.

The North Node in the Second House or in Taurus

Those with this placement need to develop a sense of identity and self-worth. Becoming aware of what they value and want, and creating or building something that reflects that is important for them. These individuals need to build something that is of tangible value and earn their own way with their talents. Financial self-sufficiency is important. This placement indicates the need to develop or refine a talent. The life task may involve developing or using a specific skill or talent. The talent may or may not be an artistic one depending on the rest of the chart. With this placement, the focus is on self-development, self-sufficiency, and self-reliance, as it is with the North Node in the first house or in Aries, and either enhancing the individual's resources, or using resources already developed, to produce something of merit.

The North Node in the Third House or in Gemini

Those with this placement are learning to analyze and think logically. Open-mindedness and attention to facts are important to balance intolerance and blind faith in former lifetimes. They also need to get out of their "ivory tower" and learn to live in society. In this lifetime, they are learning to listen to others and to communicate the wisdom they gained in their many lifetimes as seekers and philosophers. Their challenge is putting their understanding into concrete terms that others can understand. The life task is likely to involve either the accumulation of knowledge or the dispensing of it by teaching, writing, or speaking. Whether it concerns learning or teaching depends on the individual's development and intellectual resources. In any event, the life task will use and develop the individual's powers of reason and ability to communicate.

The North Node in the Fourth House or in Cancer

Those with this placement are exploring and developing the personal side of life: home, family, feelings, and caring for others. Home and family may have been neglected in former lifetimes in deference to work or to achieving goals. This placement attempts to balance this by focusing attention on the personal sphere. This lifetime is one of caring for others and being cared for. They are learning to nurture, nourish, and support others, and to be more aware of feelings—both their own and other people's. They need to learn to be vulnerable and show how they feel, and not try to control situations, which is what they are used to doing. If the personal sphere continues to be neglected, these individuals are likely to find themselves struggling with their work until they come to terms with this imbalance. The life task is likely to involve aspects of themselves that are being developed through their personal, emotional life, and may involve someone in their immediate family. It also may involve psychic work or work with the emotions or the unconscious.

The North Node in the Fifth House or in Leo

In former lifetimes, people with this placement relied on intellectual objectivity and a scientific approach, usually to the detriment of their own playfulness, spontaneity, and self-expression. They spent their time in intellectual pursuits, divorced from the juiciness and fun of life. Now they need to follow their heart and put matters of the heart over matters of the head. This is a lifetime for learning to love personally and not only universally, as they did in the past. They also need to develop their individuality and go after what they want rather than put their energy behind other people's dreams or group efforts, as they did in former lifetimes. They were the ones who followed the lead of others and supported their causes. Now it is time for self-development, creativity, self-expression, love, fun, play, and joy. Children, creativity, entertainment, games, or romance are likely to be important to the life task.

The North Node in the Sixth House or in Virgo

Those with this placement spent many lifetimes secluded from the world in monasteries, prisons, or asylums; lost in visions, drugs, meditation, dreams, or creativity; or dependent and helpless. From these experiences, they developed their compassion, imagination, and psychic sensitivity. Now they need to develop practical skills and the ability to handle day-to-day obligations. They need to learn to be in the world and to embrace routines and mundane responsibilities. Their challenge is to find a way to apply their compassion and sensitivity practically in the world to serve others.

The sixth house and Virgo pertain to self-development through service to others. The North Node's placement here indicates a life task involving service, which may include menial service. Because the sixth house and Virgo also rule health and diet, another possibility is work in the healing professions, particularly those related to physical healing. It also could refer to a life task that requires analysis, attention to detail, organization, or craftsmanship.

The North Node in the Seventh House or in Libra

Those with this placement need to use the confidence, courage, self-assertion, and leadership skills they developed in former lifetimes to encourage, support, and empower others, and to create harmony and peace among people. The life task might involve counseling, consulting, diplomacy, mediation, beauty, or the arts. They might help others fight their battles or work for peace or create more beauty in the world rather than fighting for themselves, as they did in their many lifetimes as a warrior. Rather than focusing on themselves and their own needs, this is a lifetime of being helpful to others. They need to become aware of the needs of others and learn to cooperate and share. In other lifetimes, they explored their own power and gave themselves the gift of self-development; now they are learning the power of giving to others. They are learning to be more selfless. They are here to empower others rather than themselves, and in so doing magnetize to them the love and attention they long for. Life will bring them opportunities for relationships because that is the means for their development in this lifetime. This placement indicates that relationships will serve a primary role in their growth. It may be that the life task will be accomplished through relationships or through a specific partnership.

The North Node in the Eighth House or in Scorpio

Those with this placement are shifting from material values to spiritual values, from ownership to joint ownership, and from a focus on self-development to partnership. In this lifetime, they aren't meant to accumulate for themselves alone but to share their wealth and work with others to further their security. They are here to support others, to help them build something, and to manifest their dreams. They can get rich by joining their talents and resources with others, but not alone. The life task is likely to use their excellent insight and talent for getting to the bottom of things, and may relate to psychology, the occult, research, or detective work. Banking, investments, and insurance are other possibilities. These are all ways they can join with others to improve their financial condition. The life task may also involve work related to growth, sex, healing, change, crisis intervention, reform, death, or transformation. They thrive on the potential for personal growth provided by crises, emergencies, and brushes with death. This placement also entails growth through relationships, especially those requiring intimacy, sexuality, or any sharing of resources. With this placement, the life task may entail either a business partnership or an intimate partnership.

The North Node in the Ninth House or in Sagittarius

Those with this placement need to learn to go beyond logic and trust their intuition. Their tendency from past lives is to seek answers from books and other people. In this lifetime, however, they need to learn to go within for answers. They are learning to trust themselves, find their own truth, and speak it. They are learning to communicate higher truths, not facts. This is a lifetime devoted to spiritual questing. Their life task may relate to bringing the truth they uncover to others through the ministry, the law, teaching, writing, speaking, publishing, psychic readings, or channeling. Many with this placement feel a sense of mission. They are here to provide inspiration, hope, faith, and a spiritual perspective. They see the big picture and are driven to share it with others. Spending time in nature refreshes them, where they are able to quiet their minds and contact their higher guidance. Foreign travel is another means by which they broaden themselves, expand their consciousness, and develop their understanding of life.

The North Node in the Tenth House or in Capricorn

This placement indicates the need to be involved in the world and in a career. Those with this placement need to learn to set goals and achieve them. They are learning to take responsibility for their lives rather than depend on others for their care and identity, as they did in former lifetimes. The focus now is on self-sufficiency and self-development through a career. The life task will develop their ability to manage and lead, and use the sensitivity and attunement to others that they developed in previous lifetimes. In this lifetime, they must be the one who takes charge. In the past, their tendency was to manipulate people with their emotions. Now they are learning to control and manage situations instead of people, and to balance their emotions with rational thought. The career is likely to be central to the life task and may even be identical to it.

The North Node in the Eleventh House or in Aquarius

Those with this placement need to place humanitarian concerns over their own personal desires and drives. They have creative talents, leadership skills, a strong will, passion, and determination from previous lifetimes, which they need to use in this one to further a cause or the collective good. Their own personal will needs to be made subordinate to the group or put to use by the group for the good of all. They are learning to cooperate with others to manifest their own dreams or the ideals of a group. The life task is likely to be involved with a cause, a group endeavor, new ideas, science, technology, astrology, or computers. It is likely to use and further develop their rational mind and objectivity. The gifts they have to offer the world are their idealism, dreams, originality, inventions, new ideas, future vision, and fresh perspective.

The North Node in the Twelfth House or in Pisces

Those with this placement are developing their spiritual awareness and understanding. They are pursuing spiritual truth, which usually requires some solitude. Their search may result in their becoming spiritual healers or teachers, psychotherapists, psychics, artists, musicians, monks, or nuns. Their life task might involve working with the unconscious, dreams, meditation, or altered states of consciousness. Another possibility is working with the mentally ill or in a hospital or institution, or serving humanity some other way. They are here to bring the spiritual dimension into everyday life. Their gifts are imagination, creativity, insight, intuition, inspiration, and spiritual understanding. They are learning to see the larger picture and to trust that a higher purpose is at work in life. This will balance their past-life tendency to worry and get lost in details. They are also learning to get answers through their intuition rather than through rational analysis, as they did in former lifetimes. When the North Node is here, sometimes the life task relates to balancing a karmic debt.

Here is a summary of the qualities that are likely to be used and strengthened when the North Node is placed there.

The North Node in Aries

initiative, assertiveness, independence, leadership, individuality, self-reliance, self-sufficiency, self-direction, courage

The North Node in Taurus

stalwart effort, patience, loyalty, self-reliance, self-sufficiency, resourcefulness, practicality, financial and business acumen, artistic ability

The North Node in Gemini

intelligence, communication and writing ability, logical analysis, a love of learning

The North Node in Cancer

sensitivity, compassion, empathy, intuition, kindness, ability to nurture

The North Node in Leo

leadership, will power, self-confidence, playfulness, creativity, self-expression, individuality, managerial skills

The North Node in Virgo

devotion to service, discrimination, practicality, attention to detail, efficiency, organization, analysis

The North Node in Libra

selflessness, fairness, sharing, cooperation, mediation, diplomacy, skill in relating one-on-one, awareness of other people's needs, an appreciation of beauty and the arts

The North Node in Scorpio

capacity for self-transformation, financial acumen, ability to be intimate and share resources, self-discipline, psychological insight, inner strength, passion, intensity of purpose, strong will, ability to deal with crises

The North Node in Sagittarius

understanding, faith, wisdom, intuition, vision

The North Node in Capricorn

self-discipline, ambition, hard work, responsibility, reliability, self-sufficiency, practicality, initiative, leadership

The North Node in Aquarius

innovation, inventiveness, originality, altruism, humanitarianism, tolerance, cooperation, objectivity

The North Node in Pisces

devotion to service, intuition, imagination, creativity, compassion, idealism, spiritual awareness and understanding

The characteristics listed above apply to the method in which the life task is carried out. These characteristics are likely to be used in other areas, too, but they are particularly important to the life task. Generally, both the characteristics of the North Node's sign and the characteristics of the most developed sign or signs in the chart will be used in the life task.

THE LIFE LESSON

Just as the life task can be seen in the chart, so can the life lesson. Three kinds of lessons contribute to the life lesson:

1. those related to a karmic debt (if one exists);

2. those necessary for human evolution; and

3. those needed to balance negative patterns established in former lifetimes.

In the first chapter, we saw how the karmic debt might be read in the chart. In the next chapter, we will see what basic lessons of human evolution each sign describes. In this section, we will see how Saturn and the South Node describe the third type of lesson, those serving to balance entrenched negative patterns from the past. Keep in mind that all three varieties of lessons contribute to one central lesson that will be referred to as the life lesson or life challenge. Each life has a life lesson that encompasses these three types of lessons.

The life lesson can be read in the chart by synthesizing the South Node, Saturn, and the themes. These chart factors describe one life challenge or, less commonly, two or three related ones. If more than one challenge exists, the same past-life experience is likely to have been responsible for them all.

The stressful aspects, particularly the squares, are one other source of information useful in confirming the life lesson. They are important because they often depict the internal conflicts that are part of the life challenge. Planets that are square each other act as foils to each other and demand that issues be faced. The issues these aspects bring to light, especially the aspects between the outer planets and the personal planets, often fit with those of Saturn, the South Node, and the themes.

Saturn and the South Node both portray negative patterns from the past, usually related, that may thwart the life task. Saturn points to a fear or an issue from a former lifetime that needs overcoming, while the South Node depicts characteristics or tendencies developed in former lifetimes that may interfere with growth or with accomplishing the life task.

When we interpret the South Node or Saturn, or any other chart factor, we have to synthesize its sign, its house, the aspects to it and their houses and signs, and the house it rules. Generally, Saturn and the South Node's sign indicate problems with that sign. However, which characteristics are a problem and to what degree vary with soul age and other influences.

Although both Saturn's sign and the South Node's are likely to be problematic, this will be true in different ways and for different reasons. The South Node's sign is often a sign with which we have had so much experience that we may have neglected its opposite sign (or other signs) and become entrenched in some of the South Node sign's negative expressions while developing its gifts. Even so, some older souls manage to have the gifts of the South Node's sign without its negative tendencies. The same could be said about the North Node's sign: how it will be expressed depends on past-life experience with that sign. The North Node's sign may be relatively undeveloped or, in an older soul, it may represent gifts.

Regardless of the individual's level of development, the South Node's sign represents qualities we must learn to express positively and integrate with the North Node's positive qualities. I highly recommend reading what Tracy Marks has written on the Moon's nodes and how to integrate the signs and houses involved. Since I cannot say it better than she already has, I refer you to her book *The Astrology of Self-Discovery* to supplement the information in this chapter.

The South Node's house, like its sign, represents an area of life in which we may have been overly focused to the detriment of other areas, making it necessary now to focus on the area of life in which the North Node is found. Here again, depending on the individual's development and experiences, the degree to which this area of life is a problem will vary. For anyone, the message is to focus on the North Node's house and integrate the area of life represented by the South Node into the North Node's affairs.

Saturn's house or sign represents a fear that needs healing or a lesson that needs to be learned or both. The rest of the chart will provide clues about which interpretation applies. For example, someone with Saturn in the fifth house or in Leo may have difficulty expressing himself because in a former lifetime he met with violence or death for doing so. In this lifetime, he will have to work to overcome this fear. The remainder of his chart is likely to be strong in fire to help him. Someone else with Saturn in the fifth house or in Leo might have misused his powers of self-expression in a former lifetime. In that case, Saturn represents lessons concerning self-expression. The remainder of his chart will reflect water, rather than fire, to develop sensitivity and compassion.

In summary, Saturn's house:

a) represents an area of life in which we will meet our karma or lessons. We are likely to be tested in this area to help us learn a lesson needed to balance a past act, or perhaps just to learn something. Whatever we need to learn will be delivered through this area of life. Consequently, we may be asked to take on added burdens or responsibilities in this area. These challenges also may have been freely chosen by an older soul in the hope of accelerating his or her evolution.

b) *may* represent an area of life in which fear has developed because of a negative experience in a past life. Life is likely to bring us what we need for our healing and reward any efforts to overcome our fear. It will be important to try to overcome any fears in this area.

c) represents an area of life related to the career and possibly to the life task if they are related.

Saturn's sign:

a) represents a weakness or negative quality that has caused problems in previous lifetimes and which may cause problems in this one as well (e.g., Saturn in Leo may represent a misuse of one's will. Saturn in Virgo may represent an overly critical attitude). The negative quality, which may be mild or extreme, may create the need for further trials or lessons. What makes interpretation difficult is that the characteristic may be any one of the many negative expressions of Saturn's sign.

b) *may* represent a fear based on a bad experience in a past life and the negative quality that developed, or a positive quality that failed to develop as a result of that fear. The bad experience may or may not be related to Saturn's sign, but the results affect the expression of Saturn's sign (e.g., Saturn in Aries may represent not being able to take action because acting assertively in the past had negative results. Saturn in Pisces may indicate a fear of letting go from formerly having lost oneself to mental illness).

c) represents qualities related to the career and possibly to the life task if they are related.

Saturn's sign and house must be examined with these various possibilities in mind. The only way to determine which role or roles Saturn is playing in a chart is to examine the other chart factors and use your intuition.

SATURN AND THE SOUTH NODE IN THE SIGNS

The sign in which Saturn or the South Node is found describes negative traits from former lifetimes, which may thwart the life task. The categories for Saturn in the signs below correspond to the three possible meanings (a, b, and c) mentioned above.

Saturn in Aries

Weaknesses: misuse of one's will, domineering, uncooperative, self-centered, selfish, impatient, impulsive

Fears: fear of self-assertion, lack of courage

Career/Life Task: work related to science, inventions, athletics, pioneering, or the military

Saturn in Taurus

Weaknesses: misuse of one's resources, wasteful, greedy, miserly, materialistic, hedonistic, stubborn, narrow-minded

Fears: fear of poverty, hoarding

Career/Life Task: work related to business, banking, agriculture, architecture, or the arts

Saturn in Gemini

Weaknesses: misuse of one's power of communication and influence

Fears: fear of expressing oneself, feelings of intellectual inferiority, shyness

Career/Life Task: work related to communication, transportation, writing, or teaching

Saturn in Cancer

Weaknesses: insecure, hypersensitive, overly-dependent, self-protective, withdrawn

Fears: fear of abandonment, fear of intimacy, fear of expressing one's feelings or emotional needs, blocks to giving and receiving love

Career/Life Task: work related to feelings, the home, real estate, food, children, women, or caring for others

Saturn in Leo

Weaknesses: improper use of one's will or authority, dictatorial, dogmatic, rigid

Fears: lack of confidence and self-esteem, fear of expressing oneself (including creatively), fear of giving love

Career/Life Task: work related to entertainment, speculation, children, teaching, or creativity

Saturn in Virgo

Weaknesses: overly critical or analytical, worrying, self-deprecating, subservient, repressed sexuality

Fears: fear of illness, fear of asserting oneself, hypochondria, compulsions, feelings of inferiority

Career/Life Task: work related to analysis, service, health, healing, or diet

Saturn in Libra

Weaknesses: sacrificing oneself to relationships, dependency, clinging, lack of identity

Fears: fear of relationships, fear of rejection, fear of being hurt

Career/Life Task: work related to counseling, justice, beauty, or the arts

Saturn in Scorpio

Weaknesses: misuse of one's power, controlling, manipulative, fanatic, ruthless, unforgiving

Fears: fear of intimacy, insecurity about sexuality, lack of trust

Career/Life Task: work related to sex, death, taxes, finances, research, healing, crises, psychology, or the occult

Saturn in Sagittarius

Weaknesses: intolerance, dogmatism, over-zealousness, self-righteousness, blind faith

Fears: fear of travel and exploration, a lack of faith or guiding philosophy

Career/Life Task: work related to foreign countries or foreign travel, publishing, religion, the law, teaching, or philosophy

Saturn in Capricorn

Weaknesses: misuse of one's power and influence, motivated by greed and power, dictatorial, unscrupulous, rigid

Fears: fear of failure, lack of ambition, fear of authority

Career/Life Task: work related to business, government, management, organization

Saturn in Aquarius

Weaknesses: dogmatism, intolerance, coldness, insensitivity

Fears: fear of joining in, feeling alienated, lonely, or isolated

Career/Life Task: work related to social reform, humanitarian efforts, science, inventions, technology, astrology, new ideas, or groups

Saturn in Pisces

Weaknesses: hypersensitive, overly emotional, anxious, paranoid, neurotic, moody, depressed, negative

Fears: fear of feelings, repressed feelings, fear of the subconscious and the supernatural, fear of losing one's mind, lack of faith or spiritual orientation

Career/Life Task: work related to healing, mental health, hospitals, institutions, spirituality, creativity, or service

The South Node in Aries

selfishness, self-absorption, self-centeredness, lack of awareness of other people's needs, lack of cooperation, contentiousness, aggressiveness, impulsiveness, impatience

The South Node in Taurus

hedonism, attachment to pleasures and comforts, materialistic, greedy or miserly, lacking vision and a spiritual outlook, possessiveness, stubbornness, resistance to change, inability to let go of things

The South Node in Gemini

lack of focus, indecisiveness, superficiality, lack of perspective and a philosophical approach, changing too easily, not following through

The South Node in Cancer

dependency, lack of an independent identity, lack of objectivity, moodiness, depression, emotionality, insecurity

The South Node in Leo

egotism, pride, self-absorption, domination of others, willfulness, need to have one's own way, stubbornness, blind passion, overly dramatic

The South Node in Virgo

overly analytical and critical, judgmental, workaholism, immersion in work and mundane activities, perfectionism, overemphasis on detail, anxiety, worry

The South Node in Libra

dependency on relationships for fulfillment, indecisiveness, lack of an independent identity, overly compromising and compliant

The South Node in Scorpio

losing oneself in others, dependency, going to extremes, creating crises and dramas

The South Node in Sagittarius

losing oneself in impractical abstractions, wandering from place to place or from idea to idea, accepting ideas without sufficient logical analysis, narrow-mindedness, dogmatism, self-righteousness

The South Node in Capricorn

ruled by ambition, greedy, power-seeking, social-climbing, emotionally repressed, coldness, harshness, selfishness, controlling, dominating

The South Node in Aquarius

being a follower, lack of passion and emotion, emotional detachment, impractical idealism

The South Node in Pisces

escapism, irresponsibility, impracticality, over-sensitivity, passivity, dependency, over-emotionality, irrationality, confusion, lack of discrimination, being a victim

SATURN IN THE HOUSES AND SIGNS

When reading the interpretations that follow of Saturn in the houses and signs, please understand that not everyone's lessons are a result of negative actions in past lives. An older soul may choose a particular challenge for growth rather than out of the need to balance a past act or attitude. Also keep in mind that any karma being balanced may be nearly released, which would result in only a mild manifestation of the lesson. So although the worst possibilities must be mentioned, most people do not experience them. Finally, take comfort in knowing that no one is alone in having made mistakes. Each of us has made nearly every mistake imaginable in our efforts to evolve.

Saturn's house and sign are also indicators of the career as well as the life task if they are the same. However, this information is not included in the following descriptions.

Saturn in the First House or in Aries

This placement may indicate a fear of self-expression or self-assertion resulting from a past-life experience in which this caused pain or suffering. This fear manifests as feelings of insecurity, lack of confidence or courage, shyness, awkwardness, and an inability to assert oneself. The cure lies in involvement with others, since this provides opportunities for self-assertion and gaining confidence. Solitary activity only reinforces the individual's self-focus and fear of others.

This placement may also indicate an abuse of will in a former lifetime, which is being balanced by frustrations and delays in attaining one's goals. The individual's will is thwarted, and through these frustrations, humility and empathy are acquired.

When Saturn is conjunct the Ascendant in the first house, it often coincides with a difficult birth and the resultant sense that the world is not a safe or welcoming place. This contributes to a pessimistic and defeatist attitude, which may become a self-fulfilling prophecy. These individuals have to fight to overcome their negativity and to assert their will toward their goals.

Saturn in the Second House or in Taurus

With this placement, there may be a fear of poverty and a sense of never having enough resulting from an experience of scarcity in a past life. Of course, this could also be the result of being born into poverty in the current lifetime. Everyone has experienced or will experience scarcity at some time. For some, this placement represents a choice to work through this issue now. Others may be balancing a past life of hoarding or materialism. Both experiences—greed and poverty—are likely to manifest as a drive to accumulate wealth, resulting in lessons about what is of true value. People with this placement are bound to learn that no amount of money can buy security or a sense of self-worth, which can only come from within. These lessons may be delivered by having great wealth and losing it, by experiencing the emptiness of material satisfaction, or through frustrations and delays in attaining it.

Saturn in the Third House or in Gemini

This placement may symbolize a number of different fears originating either in a past life or this one. Those with this placement may have a fear of traveling resulting from a transportation accident or tragedy that occurred while traveling. They might be afraid of expressing themselves, speaking to a group, or learning as a result of being punished for talking, reading, or learning. These fears may manifest as stuttering, shyness, poor performance in school, or a sense of inadequacy about themselves and their mental capabilities.

Many with this placement work hard to develop their intellectual and verbal abilities in an attempt to conquer their sense of shame and feelings of inferiority. Once they have overcome their handicap, many excel in scholarly tasks. They can be excellent teachers because of their compassion and understanding. They turn their weakness into a strength, which is common with issues surrounding Saturn.

Others may have misused their power of communication or prevented others from learning or speaking in a past life and will meet with lessons to balance this. Sometimes, balancing is accomplished by restricting the individual's ability to communicate, which might manifest as speech or hearing problems, learning problems, or even mental retardation.

Saturn in the Fourth House or in Cancer

This placement of Saturn often symbolizes the need to address a difficulty with a family member stemming from a former lifetime. Releasing this karma may be a significant part of the life challenge. There may be fear surrounding the relationship and a sense of burden and responsibility resulting in one or the other person appearing emotionally cool and distant. Nonetheless, the responsibility cannot be avoided. If it is, the two will meet again under similar circumstances until the responsibility is accepted and fulfilled. The planets and signs involved provide additional information about this relationship and to whom it is referring.

When this placement does not represent a karmic relationship, it symbolizes a challenge chosen by the individual that usually manifests as insufficient emotional support from a parent or parents. The home life might be disturbed by divorce or the death of a parent, burdened by a lack of resources or sickness, or simply lacking in warmth and emotional closeness. This leaves the individual emotionally wounded and feeling unloved. As a result, he or she craves the protection and emotional connection that were lacking, but has difficulty trusting others and opening up emotionally to them.

There are many possible reasons for choosing such a challenge in one's upbringing. In almost every case, it develops compassion and an appreciation for the importance of family and of properly caring for children. This side of life might have been neglected or undervalued in previous lifetimes, or the individual might have abandoned a family and is now experiencing how that feels.

Saturn in the Fifth House or in Leo

This placement indicates a fear of self-expression. This manifests, like Saturn in the first house or in Aries, as a lack of confidence, courage, self-assertion, energy, and enthusiasm. The fear may be rooted in a past-life experience of repression or oppression. Those with this placement may have misused their power or self-expression, so now they are especially cautious in these matters.

For people with this placement, the world is a serious and foreboding place. They find it hard to play, be spontaneous, and enjoy life. They are often stiff, shy, or awkward. Their creativity may be blocked or their creative products unfulfilling. They struggle with feelings of inadequacy and being unloved, and have difficulty expressing affection, though they are hungry for both affection and recognition, and demand them from others. Thus, they bring rejection and heartbreak on themselves, making it all the more difficult for them to love themselves. Nevertheless, that is what they need to learn to do. They must realize their own significance and individuality.

This placement may also indicate a karmic debt owed to a child or to children, resulting in responsibility, burdens, or work related to children. Sometimes it coincides with a reluctance or inability to have children. Restrictions on having children could serve a karmic purpose or serve to focus energy in another direction, one that is more appropriate to the life task.

Saturn in the Sixth House or in Virgo

This placement of Saturn may indicate a lingering fear of illness from a past life that may motivate the individual to pay special attention to health and diet. Consequently, it is common in the charts of health practitioners. Many with this placement are learning about the connection between the mind and the body.

This placement also often correlates with health difficulties, which may be either mental or physical. The signs and any other planets involved will identify the likely areas of weakness. The illness or difficulty may be related to balancing a karmic debt, which may or may not be associated with health matters. It could also represent a freely chosen challenge. The reason for the illness or difficulty cannot be determined from the chart alone. Its seriousness can range from mild and relatively nonproblematic to life threatening. The transits will tell of its possible onset and course, which may be either chronic or acute. On the other hand, this placement might just be teaching the importance of diet, hygiene, and proper care of the body, which is one of life's basic lessons.

Another important lesson for those with this placement is service. Many people with Saturn in the sixth house or in Virgo find themselves in subservient positions or performing menial work. Limitations, frustrations, and discontentment with work are common. They might be stuck in an unsatisfying job or chafing against the boredom of an endless daily routine. This may be serving to teach them humility and the value of service, and to balance any negative attitudes toward work and routine. They need to establish organization and a routine in their lives and learn to embrace even the most mundane of tasks.

Saturn in the Seventh House or in Libra

With this placement, fear originating from abandonment or loneliness in a past life may be responsible for discomfort and difficulties in relationships. Those with this placement long for relationships but are afraid of being hurt. Consequently, they may withhold themselves from others or choose partners who are safe (e.g., ones who are below them or who have problems). Their anticipation of being hurt or rejected by others can become a self-fulfilling prophesy. They tend to form relationships that are restricting, burdensome, disappointing, or unloving. Many are attracted to more serious types or those who are older and can provide the stability, faithfulness, and money they need to feel safe.

These individuals are forced to face certain important lessons in love and to learn to cope with aloneness. Their struggles with relationships often result in a drive to understand people and relationships. They take relationships very seriously and may even study them or become experts on the subject. Many become counselors or work with people one-on-one. They also may marry at an older age, which allows them to take more time to learn about relationships.

This placement may also indicate a karmic relationship with their mate or a career in which a partnership is crucial. On the other hand, it might serve to focus their energy in directions other than relationships by delaying or blocking them.

Saturn in the Eighth House or in Scorpio

Those with this placement often have a fear of intimacy and difficulty merging with another. They may also have difficulty giving or receiving in relationships. This difficulty may stem from betrayal or some other misfortune in love in a past life or in the current one. The problem might have its origin in a family that is abusive, cold, or emotionally disconnected. They crave union with another but fear the emotions that might be unleashed if they do, such as passion, jealousy, or rage. These individuals not only fear sharing themselves emotionally with others (and may not even know how) but sexually as well. Sexual dysfunction or overcompensating for their fears by being promiscuous is a possibility with this placement. However, difficulties manifest more often as emotional trials, such as unfaithfulness and betrayal. Despite these challenges, the individual must learn to trust and share more intimately with another.

Misuse or abuse of power in a former lifetime and the need for lessons to correct this is another possibility. Those with this placement could become victims of sexual abuse or other forms of violence or emotional wounding, perhaps to balance karma. Such challenges may be chosen to motivate individuals to learn the deeper secrets of psychology and of their own emotional makeup. It necessitates healing and going within, which may be part of the soul's growth in this lifetime.

Another possible challenge is around other people's money. There may be obstacles in procuring a divorce settlement, an inheritance, or tax moneys. This, too, may be karmic. Finally, it may be that a karmic debt is owed to, or has willingly been taken on by, a romantic or business partner. If that is the case, the individual may be burdened financially by a partnership.

Saturn in the Ninth House or in Sagittarius

Those with this placement may have experienced mental oppression, dogmatism, or a restriction of personal freedom in a former lifetime from religious, legal, governmental, or educational institutions or from family members. They may experience these things in this lifetime. As a result, they may have lost faith or claim to believe in nothing. Many feel disillusioned by the faith in which they were brought up, finding it inadequate to answer life's questions or simply too oppressive to be useful. These individuals need to discover their own truth and invest energy in compiling a belief system that works for them. They may study law, religion, government, or philosophy in an effort to uncover the understanding they seek. Once they have, they often become teachers of these subjects.

This placement may also indicate intolerance, bigotry, dogmatism, or oppression that needs to be balanced. One way this is done is for the individual to experience the same bigotry or oppression that he or she has engaged in, or the individual might be betrayed or let down by a spiritual leader or religion. More positively, it might be balanced through exposure to those of other cultures and beliefs, which hopefully will broaden the individual's understanding. Even this could be challenging, as it rocks the individual's cherished beliefs.

Saturn in the Tenth House or in Capricorn

This position may indicate a fear of success, of one's own power, or of public humiliation stemming from a fall from a high social position in a previous lifetime. People with this placement may have abused the power that society invested in them in a past life and must be careful not to repeat the mistake. On the other hand, the fear of failure, intense ambition, need to be important, and sense of inadequacy of this placement may be a response to a father or mother who is critical, demanding, and cold. To succeed, these individuals will have to overcome their self-doubts and the resulting inertia. They will be wise to refrain from using unethical means for attaining power, and from abusing the power they do achieve. If they don't, disgrace or a fall is likely.

Those with this position of Saturn will probably have to work hard to attain and maintain their social status, as it often brings obstacles, delays, disappointments, or a lack of opportunity in the career. However, with due caution, discipline, hard work, and humility, great things can be achieved. The individual needs to transform any greed for power into a drive for serving the larger social order. That is the route to the recognition and respect that he or she so desires.

Saturn in the Eleventh House or in Aquarius

In a former lifetime, those with this placement may have been outcast by a group or a community, or rejected by peers. This may have left emotional scars, making it hard now for them to make friends or feel like they belong. As a result, they may need special understanding and encouragement when they are young to build their confidence and help them overcome their shyness and sense of social isolation. This placement may also indicate rejection or ostracism by others in this lifetime and leave similar emotional scars, especially if it occurs when the individual is very young.

Because of their fear of rejection and aversion to groups, these individuals may be attracted to a rural or reclusive lifestyle, one in which they can be away from people and the challenge to their self-esteem that is aroused by social situations. To cover up their insecurity, they might pretend to be superior or tell themselves that it is because they are special that they don't fit in.

A more constructive use of this placement is for them to become involved with a group or a cause. This is one way for them to overcome their sense of inferiority and isolation. Only by facing our fears can we overcome them, and this is one fear that is easy to run from. These individuals need to become involved with others, express themselves within groups, and assume leadership for the common good.

Another possibility is that friends will be a catalyst for their growth and an avenue through which they meet their karma in some way. They may be asked to take on responsibilities as a result of a friendship, or friendships may be burdensome or challenging. With this placement, the people they meet in groups and with whom they form friendships may be people they knew in previous lifetimes. This position may also indicate working with a friend.

Saturn in the Twelfth House or in Pisces

Many with this placement of Saturn are drawn to serving those confined in institutions. This may be to assuage their own fear of being confined, dependent, incapacitated, mentally ill, or helpless from having experienced these conditions in a former lifetime. Their service in these areas may also be a way for them to repay service they received from society when they were dependent or incapacitated. Those with this placement, especially those who have been mentally ill in the past, are afraid of being engulfed by their emotions and of losing their identity. They fear what lurks below the surface of their conscious mind. They will work hard to avoid these possibilities by paying their dues to society and serving those whose condition they fear most. Their desire to serve in these areas also comes from the compassion they developed from having been confined, mentally ill, or incapacitated in a former lifetime.

Another possibility is a karmic debt. Many with this placement feel a deep-seated guilt and a sense of obligation to others or to society, which may be based on a karmic debt. They may have taken advantage of the mentally ill, the sick, or others who are weak or vulnerable. A common means of balancing this debt is through service, particularly of a psychological or spiritual nature. Some make penance by becoming healers or monks or nuns, for instance. Those with this placement might need to experience their own helplessness and vulnerability through circumstances that inhibit their ability to function within society. Isolation, dependency, hospitalization, institutionalization, and incarceration are the most extreme possibilities for this lesson. Through these experiences, we learn compassion. We also learn the necessity of having to submit our own will to a higher one. These experiences serve to break down our ego and help us to realize the Self beyond the personal self. Service and a willingness to explore their depths and experience unity consciousness are what is being asked of these individuals.

THE SOUTH NODE IN THE HOUSES AND SIGNS

The South Node in the First House or in Aries

The South Node in the first house or in Aries indicates an emphasis on self-development in past lives. As a result, those with this placement may be more adept at pursuing their own goals than at relationships. They have had many lifetimes as warriors, athletes, adventurers, and pioneers, where initiative, leadership, and independent action were important. In this lifetime, they are learning to relate to others, to cooperate, and to share. In the past, they were used to earning love through their achievements rather than through attending to the needs of others. Now they must learn to give to others what they need. To do this, they will have to become more sensitive to the needs of others and learn to communicate with them. They also will have to learn to be a team player. Because they are afraid that others will take away from their identity or cramp their style, they have a tendency to be self-protective and defensive, which must be overcome. In this lifetime, they will be prevented from being too independent and required to learn to relate to others. If self-development is pursued for its own sake, it will be discouraged. The independence, strength, and self-assurance they developed in previous lifetimes are to be used to further a partnership or the welfare of others rather than their own personal goals.

The South Node in the Second House or in Taurus

In previous lifetimes, those with this placement were farmers, landowners, bankers, and builders who contributed in practical and tangible ways to society. In the past, wealth, pleasure, and comfort were their goals. They need to develop self-discipline now, which will balance their tendency toward self-indulgence and excessive pleasure-seeking. In this lifetime, they will be discouraged from focusing on material acquisition or self-development in deference to sharing their material resources and applying their energies to understanding and enriching their partnerships. They are learning to share and merge their resources with others. This time, they need to build something in conjunction with a partner, not alone. Their ability to sustain themselves will be used in this lifetime to sustain others and to provide themselves with the freedom to seek greater understanding and self-awareness. One of their challenges is letting go. They are here to learn to do that and to embrace change and its potential for self-transformation. Their resistance to change is one of the greatest stumbling blocks to their life task. Their stubbornness, attachment to doing things their own way, and their resistance to getting help from others also need to be overcome. They have a natural attunement to the physical world but now need to attune themselves to the more subtle aspects of life—to the emotional, spiritual, and psychological.

The South Node in the Third House or in Gemini

Those with this placement have had many lifetimes as teachers, writers, speakers, or reporters. They have spent many lifetimes studying other people's points of view and gathering information without concern for its purpose or meaning. Now it is time for them to form their own opinions and express their own personal view of reality. This is a lifetime for developing their intuition and getting in touch with their own inner truth. They are moving away from basing their conclusions on facts to basing them on inner knowing. In the past, an overly active and logical mind, and immersion in the details of daily life, may have prevented them from being in contact with their intuition and spiritual self. Those with this placement must learn to apply their well-oiled minds to formulating a philosophy and establishing a framework for their many facts. They will not find satisfaction in their mental activities until this shift toward understanding and philosophy is made. They need to focus on the deeper side of life.

The South Node in the Fourth House or in Cancer

Those with this placement have had many lifetimes as nurturers, heads of households, and in situations where family was central. Then, they depended on others for their security and support. Their identification with others in these lifetimes developed their emotional sensitivity and relationship skills. Now they need to get out into the world to balance these lifetimes at home. They have to learn to take care of their own needs rather than continue being caretakers or being taken care of by others. This placement indicates a need to shift focus from the personal sphere to the professional, and to contribute one's sensitivity and compassion to this greater sphere. People with this placement will be pulled toward home and family, which are viewed as less threatening than career. However, satisfaction will not be found until they accept the importance of career in their life. This will be made easier through assistance with their career and the satisfaction they will find in pursuing it.

The South Node in the Fifth House or in Leo

Those with this placement were artists, creative people, performers, leaders, and kings and queens in former lifetimes. In these lifetimes, they developed their talents and individuality and were used to receiving attention and respect from others. Now they will have to overcome their sense of being special and put these talents to use for the common good. They need to learn to work with others rather than rule or go it alone, as they did in past lives. They also need to become more objective to balance their passionate and intense approach in past lives. In this lifetime, they will have to harness their passion and well-developed will to support other people's dreams or a collective goal. Because this placement may indicate an overemphasis on self-development in past lives, these individuals will be prevented from being too self-focused and required to learn to share and cooperate with others. If self-development is pursued for its own sake or for self-aggrandizement, it will be discouraged.

The South Node in the Sixth House or in Virgo

In former lifetimes, those with this placement were doctors, nurses, and other medical practitioners. They were involved in practical service to humanity. As a result, they are skilled, precise, efficient, organized, perfectionists, and detail-oriented. They are used to using their mind and practical skills to manage life. Now they must develop their intuition and spiritual understanding. Their tendency to worry and to try to control life by compulsively ordering their environment needs to be remedied by spiritual understanding and acceptance that life is purposeful and good. In this lifetime, they need to learn to "let go and let God" and recognize that a higher plan is at work despite the chaos, imperfection, and unpredictability of life. This lifetime also calls for greater understanding about the role the mind and emotions play in physical health and healing. Also common to this placement are health problems. Besides balancing karma, health problems provide a way to learn to transcend the body and experience the spiritual dimension, which is what these individuals are here to learn.

The South Node in the Seventh House or in Libra

Those with this placement have had many lifetimes giving to others and working in tandem with them toward their goals, usually at the expense of developing their own identities and pursuing their own goals. Relationships in former lifetimes may have interfered with self-development and the development of courage, independence, and initiative. Now it is time for them to use their sensitivity to the needs of others and their excellent relationship skills to advance their own personal goals. They will be encouraged by life toward self-development and self-sufficiency, and away from dependence on others.

The South Node in the Eighth House or in Scorpio

Those with this placement tend to be dependent and overly involved in other people's lives. In former lifetimes, they were used to merging with others and, consequently, lost sight of their own separate identity. Their immersion in relationships developed their psychological insight and sensitivity to other people's needs, but now they must develop their own talents and resources and an identity separate from their relationships. They need to apply their excellent insight and relationship skills to further their own development and material progress. They need to earn their own way now. However, they will probably not find satisfaction in accumulating wealth for its own sake but for its ability to enhance their relationships and understanding of life.

The South Node in the Ninth House or in Sagittarius

Those with this placement have spent many lifetimes pursuing truth and understanding, usually at the expense of developing themselves in other ways. They do have a special spiritual and intuitive awareness as a result of these incarnations. They need to share their truth now, but they have to watch out for self-righteousness, narrow-mindedness, and the need to be right. In these lifetimes, they may have placed too much emphasis on intuitive knowing and not enough on logical analysis. Their challenge now is to learn to concretize their ideas and communicate them. They must learn to express their ideas and wisdom in a way that others can understand. Satisfaction will not come from pursuing ideas in isolation but by being in the world and sharing them with others.

The South Node in the Tenth House or in Capricorn

This placement symbolizes a former focus on career or work-related activities, possibly to the detriment of the personal sphere. Many with this placement achieved positions of authority and social prominence in previous lifetimes. They are used to repressing their feelings and instincts, and putting their goals and achievements above personal relationships. A shift of focus to the personal sphere is now required, which will allow previously neglected lessons to be learned. The areas that need their attention are home, family, feelings, the inner life, and the care of others. Life will present them with opportunities for growth through familial relationships to moderate the drive for career. Although parenthood may not be necessary, learning to nurture others is important. Those with this placement may be afraid of losing themselves in others; however, this fear is more of an excuse for avoiding relationships than a real possibility.

The South Node in the Eleventh House or in Aquarius

Those with this placement have supported humanitarian efforts or the dreams and ideals of others in former lifetimes. In this lifetime, they need to pursue their own dreams. Even though the pull may be toward following others and not taking initiative, this is a lifetime in which independent action, self-development, and creative exploration are important. Although these activities may seem frivolous and selfish to them, they are what is called for. Their task is to apply the idealism and vision they developed in former lifetimes to pursuing their own goals, developing their talents, and leading others. If they are able to do this, they can produce creative products that have value to the collective, which is often what the life task is about. This is a lifetime for standing out from the crowd and being recognized for their individuality and talents.

The South Node in the Twelfth House or in Pisces

Those with the South Node in this house or sign need to overcome their tendency to escape the world, their inclination to play the victim, their hypersensitivity, and their impracticality. They need to come out of their inner world and apply their compassion, intuition, and spiritual insight in practical service or healing work. This is a lifetime of practical service in the real world, not one of withdrawal into the world of imagination, dreams, and altered states of consciousness, so familiar to them. This placement is common for those whose life task involves physical healing as opposed to spiritual or emotional healing. However, they need to apply what they know about the spirit and the emotions in their healing or service work. As with the reversal of these nodes, for many the task is to understand the relationship between the mind and body in healing.

THE SIX NODAL AXES

The North Node and the South Node represent a polarity. Because they represent two sides of one issue, two sides of a coin, their integration leads to wholeness and balance. The goal is to integrate the nodal signs and houses, with an emphasis on the North Node as the direction and purpose for this lifetime. This integration is usually central to the life task.

Aries/Libra or First House/Seventh House Nodal Axis

This nodal axis highlights the age-old dilemma of independence versus dependence. The issue will be either that of individualization and developing oneself or of learning to share and cooperate within a partnership. The skills involved in this axis are opposite, which is not true for every axis. When the North Node is in Aries or in the first house, *being alone* develops the skills that are needed. When the North Node is in Libra or in the seventh house, *being in a relationship* develops the skills that are needed. Depending on which lesson is needed, those with this placement will spend the majority of their time either alone or in a relationship until the South Node's lesson is learned.

Taurus/Scorpio or Second House/Eighth House Nodal Axis

This is another axis associated with the dilemma of self versus others. Although it is tied to the issue of balanced involvement in relationships, this axis is more about developing one's own talents versus making a similar investment of energy in intimate relationships or in someone else's talents. This axis also concerns developing and defining one's values, with material values needing to be integrated with spiritual and interpersonal ones.

Gemini/Sagittarius or Third House/Ninth House Nodal Axis

This is the teaching axis. Those with this nodal placement have a life task involving learning or teaching, or both, depending on their development. Much time will be spent seeking, absorbing, assimilating, and disseminating knowledge or wisdom.

Cancer/Capricorn or Fourth House/Tenth House Nodal Axis

The issue represented by this nodal axis is one of career versus the personal sphere. Those with this placement often feel pulled in two directions and guilty about not being able to attend to both equally. They need to learn to balance and integrate their professional and personal lives, while paying particular attention to the matters of the North Node. People with this placement may feel especially drawn to South Node activities and may find it hard to activate the area of the North Node. However, life will present them with opportunities to do so until the activities associated with the North Node feel more natural. This axis also highlights the issue of self-sufficiency versus mutual dependence, with the need to develop more of one or the other.

Leo/Aquarius or Fifth House/Eleventh House Nodal Axis

The issue represented by this nodal placement is individuality versus group membership, and group goals versus individual goals. Those with the North Node in Aquarius or in the eleventh house are learning to subjugate their own goals to the group's or to accept the group's goals as their own. Those with the North Node in Leo or in the fifth house are exploring their own goals as a means for developing their individuality and creativity. This axis also highlights the issue of personal love versus humanitarian or altruistic love, with a greater focus on one or the other depending on the placement.

Virgo/Pisces or Sixth House/Twelfth House Nodal Axis

This placement symbolizes a life task involving service. That service often involves healing, with physical healing being more likely when the North Node is in Virgo or in the sixth house, and emotional healing being more likely when the North Node is in Pisces or in the twelfth house.

SYNTHESIZING THE INFORMATION IN THE CHART

We also need to identify the chart themes before we can understand the life task and life lesson. Each chart has several themes, symbolized by the prominent signs in the chart, but we don't stop here. Once we have found the themes, we have to synthe-size them. If we don't, we may miss the story the chart tells. The chart reveals the meaning of the person's life as it is reflected in the lessons and the life task. This is what further synthesis accomplishes.

Each theme symbolized by a sign has its lessons. Although these lessons by themselves have some significance, their real importance lies in their ability to define the major life lesson, which is derived by synthesizing all the themes' lessons. The life task is derived sim-ilarly, by synthesizing the gifts of the themes. Having a theme in the chart entitles you to either the gifts or the lessons of the sign, or a little of both depending on the sign's level of development and your former experiences.

Synthesizing the themes' lessons reveals the life challenge; synthe-sizing the themes' gifts reveals the life task; and synthesizing the themes' lessons and gifts reveals the chart's message. This information combined with information from the Moon's Nodes and Saturn completes the picture of the story told by the chart.

The soul knows what lessons are to be learned and what ener-gies are needed for the life task, and it plans the chart accordingly. When a sign needed for a particular lesson or for the life task is not available at the appointed time of reentry into life, the soul can pro-vide the energy in the chart in other ways. Choosing the needed sign as an Ascendant or putting a group of planets within the house nat-urally ruled by that sign will add that energy to the chart, as will putting the ruler of that sign on an angle. Those are the main ways of adding an energy to the chart when it is not available through the signs. So, when we are searching for the themes, we need to look at the houses and the angles as well as the signs.

Finding the Themes

The themes are found by examining the following, in order of importance:

1. The signs in which the personal planets are found, espe-cially the Sun, the Moon, and Ascendant.

The signs of the Sun, the Moon, and Ascendant always represent themes, which are likely to be supported by other factors in the chart. The signs of the other personal planets (Mercury, Venus, and Mars) may represent a theme if support exists for that theme elsewhere. If two of these personal planets are in the same sign, a theme is indicated. If a group of planets includes at least one of these personal planets, a theme is indicated. One personal planet and one nonpersonal planet in a sign are not enough to warrant a theme unless support exists elsewhere for that theme. If there is a group of nonpersonal planets in a sign, check to see if other factors support that theme.

2. The *houses* occupied by the largest number of planets, particularly the personal planets.

The signs that naturally rule the houses emphasized by planets will be strengthened. For instance, having a planet in the first house is similar to having a planet in Aries because Aries is the natural ruler of the first house.

If the planets in a house are the Sun, the Moon, or two or more of the personal planets, the sign that naturally rules that house has some significance and may represent a theme if there is support elsewhere for that theme. The amount of significance depends on which planets are in the house and how many.

Only personal planets (and usually more than one, unless that one is the Sun or the Moon) are significant enough to note. One personal planet other than the Sun or the Moon in a house may add support to an already existing theme, but by itself does not indicate a theme. The houses of Jupiter, Saturn, Uranus, Neptune, and Pluto should not be counted as adding to a theme unless there is also a personal planet contained in them.

3. The planets conjunct an angle, the Sun, or the Moon within ten degrees. The sign that those planets rule will be strengthened and may point to another theme, but by itself will not represent a theme.

4. The themes present in the major *aspects*, particularly those to the Sun, the Moon, Ascendant, or other personal planets. For example, many aspects between personal planets and Pluto reflect a Scorpio theme. Although the aspects will not define a theme without the support of other factors, checking the aspects is useful in confirming the themes and determining their strength.

The chart themes are usually easy to spot. In most cases, you will find the same signs coming up repeatedly when you use this technique.

Finding the Chart's Message

Once the themes are found, the next step is to find the themes within the themes. This entails identifying what the signs representing those themes have or do not have in common. *What the themes have in common indicate gifts and point to the life task. What they do not have in common indicate inner conflicts. The negative traits they have in common indicate a quality that needs moderation. The inner conflicts and traits that need moderation combine to create the life challenge.* Here's an example to help clarify this.

Let's suppose that we have discovered that a chart's themes are Pisces, Virgo, and Sagittarius. First, we need to identify what these signs have in common. All three signs are mutable, so the gifts and lessons will be those of the mutable signs. Pisces and Virgo also have the need to serve in common. Finally, Pisces and Sagittarius are similar in their idealism and their hunger for understanding. These similarities describe the gifts that will be used in the life task.

Next, we need to look for the differences between these signs and how they might reinforce each other's negative tendencies. Virgo and Sagittarius have different approaches to life—one is reserved and practical, and the other is outgoing and impractical. The contrasting styles of Pisces and Sagittarius reiterate a similar conflict between reserve and self-expression. These two signs also reinforce each other's tendency to be irresponsible and idealistic.

Next, this information, plus information from the Moon's nodes and Saturn, which should confirm what was uncovered by the themes, needs to be synthesized. This will give us the message of the chart. With just the information we have about the chart themes (Virgo, Pisces, and Sagittarius), we could guess that the life task will involve service using the individual's understanding. The life challenge might involve finding a practical focus and following through on it.

The themes in the next example are Libra, Virgo, Gemini, and Taurus. Libra, Virgo, and Gemini all have an intellectual orientation. (Libra and Gemini are both air signs, and Virgo and Gemini are both ruled by Mercury.) Taurus and Virgo, being earth signs, share a practical and rational approach. The elemental theme in this chart is air/earth, so the gifts and lessons are those of air/earth. This individual is likely to use his gift for turning ideas into useful products in his life task. However, concerning his life challenge, he may need help getting in touch with his emotions and intuitions (water), finding inspiration, and defining his goals (fire). Saturn and the Moon's nodes should support these conclusions and be helpful in coming to them. There should be a sense of rightness about your conclusions based on your intuition of the entire chart.

Once the themes are found and the themes within the themes are analyzed, intuition is used to arrive at the chart's message. At every stage of chart analysis, astrologers use their intuition, but nowhere is it more important than at this final stage.

The intuition is not part of the intellect, though the intellect is used to decipher and communicate intuitions. Intuitions are insights arrived at through other than conscious thought. Everyone has the capacity to intuit information. However, the level of development of this ability varies.

After doing an intellectual analysis of a chart, here are some suggestions for getting more information from it intuitively.

1. Breathe deeply and slowly for a few minutes to help you quiet your mind and relax.

2. With the chart in hand, allow your eyes to move freely around the chart. Note any impressions. These impressions may be in the form of images, words, bodily sensations, or direct knowing. Continue doing this until you feel a sense of completion signaled by a feeling of "Aha!"

3. Verify your intuitive impressions intellectually by finding further confirmation for them in the chart. Usually, the impressions fill in something you missed in your analysis. These impressions may either provide new information that helps explain what you have already uncovered or tie what you uncovered together.

The only way to learn to use your intuition is through practice. With practice, you learn which impressions you can trust. The mind and the ego have a way of interfering in the intuitive process, so the first lesson is learning to discriminate between thoughts and intuitive impressions.

The Higher Self speaks to us through a spiritual center located in the center of the chest just to the right of the actual heart. Learning to use your intuition is largely a matter of learning to tune in to the energy responses in this center. An expansive feeling can be felt in the middle of the chest when a correct conclusion is made, and a sinking or contracting sensation can be felt when incorrect. We can learn to feel the responses of this spiritual center quite easily through practice, but the mind and the body must be stilled.

Meditation stills and quiets the mind. A still mind is necessary for spiritual work because it allows intuitions to be communicated to the conscious mind. In meditation, we take time to listen to our Higher Self. This helps us live in accordance with the Plan that our Higher Self has for us. When we are in touch with this Plan, our life runs more smoothly and growth occurs more evenly.

When we are not, we find ourselves struggling against life, angry and confused about where to turn next. The answers are within if we take the time to listen.

A CASE STUDY

This study will look at the charts (see pages 72 and 73) of twins born fifteen minutes apart. The differences between their charts are not significant, yet these two people are very different—almost opposite—in how they approach the world. Given this, how does astrology explain the differences between twins who have nearly the same chart?

Twins are two people who enter life under the same energies to learn lessons and accomplish tasks related to those energies. However, one twin's lessons and task may be quite different from the other's. This is not only because the lessons and life task indicated by the themes and other chart factors are broad enough to encompass many possibilities, but also because the signs will be expressed differently depending on the amount of experience each twin has had with those signs in former lifetimes. A sign representing gifts in one chart may represent lessons for the other twin, as in this case study.

When there are outstanding differences in how twins express the signs in their charts, a difference in soul age may be the reason. When this is the case, even the most developed sign in the less advanced twin's chart may not be as developed as most of the signs in the more advanced twin's. The less advanced twin will be faced with the lessons of each of the signs in the chart and with fewer talents and resources, while the more advanced twin will have some talents and a stronger focus on the life task than on lessons.

On the other hand, the twins could be similar in soul age but have had very different past-life charts and experiences, which caused them to develop along different lines. When this is the case, their talents and lessons may be complementary: one twin's strength is the other's weakness. They might each be learning what the other has mastered. With the same family, upbringing, and age, twins are ideally situated to learn from each other. In this case study, the woman is attuned to relationships and emotions (Pisces), while the man is adept at projecting his personality in the world (Aries). Because their shortcomings are different, their growth will occur in different areas.

Varying levels of experience with each of the signs and differing soul ages explain many of the differences between twins. However, gender plays an important part as well. Whether children are born male or female in most societies has a profound effect on how they will be raised, how they will see themselves, and what opportunities will be made available to them. In our society, males find it easier to express the fire and air in their charts than the earth and water. The opposite is true for females.

Since gender and upbringing both play an important role in how the signs in the chart are expressed, it is not surprising that the soul chooses these carefully before life. Like the chart, the gender is chosen to facilitate the life task and the lessons. In this case study, the expression of the man's Arian strengths—courage, assertiveness, and enterprising action—is aided by his gender. The expression of the woman's Piscean strengths—compassion, kindness, and intuition—is aided by hers.

Let's see how two different interpretations can be arrived at from two nearly identical charts. First, we should note the differences that do exist between these two charts. The fifteen minute difference in their birth times resulted in two differences: Saturn is widely conjunct the man's Midheaven, while Neptune is conjunct the woman's. Also, Mars is in the man's fourth house, while it is in the woman's third house. This last difference may be no difference at all, since many astrologers (myself included) consider a planet within two or three degrees of a cusp to be in the next house.

These differences are not sufficient to account for the differences between these two people. What they do account for is a difference in their relationship to the world (the Midheaven): the man is motivated to succeed in a material sense, while the woman is motivated to serve. This difference gives us a clue to understanding the rest of the chart and how it functions individually for them.

Let's begin with the man. He has spent several lifetimes as an explorer, adventurer, and athlete. The courage and abilities gleaned from his many lifetimes with fiery charts are apparent in his current talents and approach to the world. Besides excelling in athletics in his youth, he has thrived on making his mark in advertising and marketing, a highly competitive industry. In his dealings with the business world, he has sought power, prestige, and the freedom to express himself in his work. Because his need for independence made it hard for him to be happy in the highly structured corporate world, he eventually struck out on his own in a career in marketing research. His drive is, and always has been, enormous, making him likely to succeed at anything he puts his mind to.

While Aries and Sagittarius clearly represent the man's attunement to the element of fire, the same cannot be said for the woman, whose fiery side became apparent only after her Saturn return. As a musician, spiritual seeker, teacher, and counselor, her attunement is to the Pisces in her chart. Unlike her brother, she has invested her energy in the more personal, emotional side of life—in relationships and caring for others. Nevertheless, as her focus has shifted toward career, her brother's has shifted toward home and family. As each twin matures, the less developed sign in their charts is beginning to blossom, a healthy sign that an integration of Pisces and Aries is taking place for both of them.

Now, let's take a look at their lessons. If any, the man's lessons with fire involve learning to moderate his energy so that he doesn't burn himself out, while the woman needs to learn to express her fire. The fire in her chart is present to balance the submissive and servile tendencies of her many lifetimes as a Pisces and a Virgo. Expressing her fire has been one of her biggest challenges. On the other hand, the man's challenge is to develop the strengths of Pisces: compassion, sensitivity, intuition, creativity, and selfless giving. Just as fire will bring strength and balance to the woman's Piscean gifts, Pisces will bring softness and balance to the man's Arian gifts. Each is learning to balance his or her gifts through experience with a less developed sign.

For both of them, integrating the positive qualities of each theme in their charts—Pisces, Gemini, Aries, and Sagittarius—will lead to accomplishing their two very different life tasks. Both of their life tasks involve communication and both will use Piscean qualities. The man is likely to use his Piscean creativity and intuition to communicate something of artistic merit, while the woman is likely to use her intuition and communication gifts to serve others, particularly their spiritual needs.

As for their life challenges and what may interfere with their life tasks, self-deprecation on her part and perfectionism on his part need to be overcome. Saturn and the South Node in Virgo symbolize both self-deprecation and perfectionism. These traits developed from very different past-life experiences.

The house in which Saturn is found, the ninth house, also represents an area of challenge for each of them but for different reasons. For the man, Saturn in the ninth house represents a lack of philosophical underpinnings. His faith has been shaken and he has difficulty committing himself to a philosophy. He is skeptical and not interested in investigating various belief systems. For the woman, the opposite is true. Although she, too, grew up under Catholicism and went through a period of disillusionment, she has spent many lifetimes, including much of this one, developing her own philosophy and understanding. Her challenge will be to put her understanding into concrete terms and make it accessible to others (the North Node in the third house) and not be dogmatic about it or remain in her "ivory tower." So, just as he can be a model for her of practical, assertive action, she can help him uncover a philosophical foundation for his action and creative expression.

Male Twin
March 15, 1951
00:55:00 AM CST
ZONE: +6:00
087W55'00"
43N02'00"

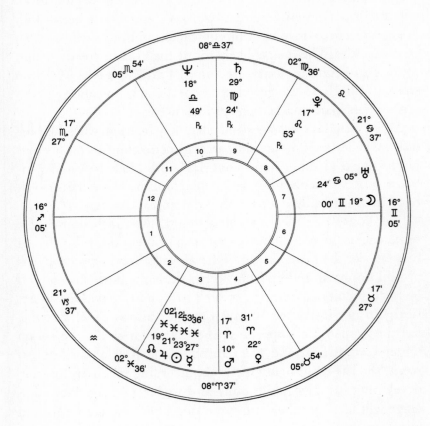

Figure 1. Male Twin

Female Twin
March 15, 1951
01:10:00 AM CST
ZONE: +6:00
087W55'00"
43N02'00"

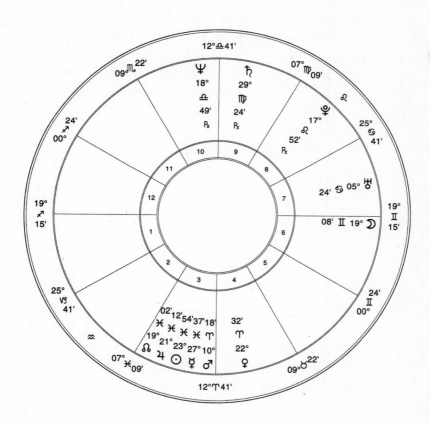

Figure 2. Female Twin

The purpose of this brief overview is not to analyze the twins' charts in detail, but to lend support to one of the fundamental premises of a psycho-spiritual approach: *The signs in our charts are at varying levels of development.* How else can the differences between twins be explained? Accepting that we have lived other lifetimes and that they influence the expression of our current chart is important if our understanding of astrology is to advance. The chart is part of a larger plan including the soul's long-range goals and the lessons of all our past lives. Without this perspective, although we can obtain valid psychological information, we cannot understand the entire person or, moreover, why that personality was chosen.

CHAPTER 3

THE EVOLUTION
OF THE SIGNS

Evolution requires a vast array of experiences and lessons. The twelve signs encompass these lessons. The lessons of each of the twelve signs must be experienced and mastered before our evolution is complete. As these lessons are being mastered, the talents and positive qualities of the sign develop. When a sign is first experienced, it will be awkwardly and more negatively expressed. Later, with more experience, its positive attributes are more easily expressed and its talents develop. Gradually, over many lifetimes, the expression of the signs evolves, yet, how this occurs is very individualized. We do not experience the signs in any set order, and we are free to choose some signs more often than others. Which signs are chosen more than others depends on the person. This allows us to focus on certain talents, lessons, or tasks.

EVOLUTION AND THE SIGNS

What follows are descriptions of the signs and how they evolve. Each sign has its own progression of growth according to its issues. As you will see, many issues evolve into strengths. While reading these descriptions, keep in mind that they apply not only to people with that Sun sign, but also to those who have that sign prominent in their chart.

Aries

This sign brings to mind images of swashbuckling pirates and freewheeling adventurers. Arians crave adventure, the novelty of new enterprise, and the excitement of risk-taking and danger. They have a need for unmitigated expression and physical activity. However, undeveloped Arians have difficulty modulating their energy and drive. They vacillate between overdrive and burnout, between ignoring their feelings and angry outbursts. Undeveloped Arians are brazen, forceful, uncouth, and outlandish. Not surprisingly, these qualities plus their independent and uncooperative nature often present problems in relationships.

The lessons of this sign include patience and perseverance. Arians usually learn patience the hard way—by making mistakes. Although patience can be a painful lesson, it is taught efficiently through the circumstances of life. By experiencing the results of their misadventures, Arians learn to control their energy and focus it. As they evolve, their urge for excitement and danger tempers and becomes focused toward a specific goal, and is often expressed in less physical ways, such as by playing the stock market, or wheeling and dealing on the corporate level.

Arians have two strengths that evolve from their love of adventure and excitement. First, they are courageous self-starters. The memory of their successful conquests, however unconscious, spurs them on to partake of life courageously and to pour their energy into new endeavors and new ideas. Their courage and daring prod them into taking on one project after another. At this level, they make excellent contributions to society with their new projects, inventions, and discoveries. Their love for life, their exuberance, and their unflagging sense of confidence are the other admirable qualities born from their love of adventure and excitement. This *joie de vivre* comes from having faced their fears and conquered them. As a result, Arians have a sense that life is good and that they are not powerless even in the face of life's most difficult blows. They have an unshakable belief in themselves and in their ability to deal with life, bolstered by an underlying sense of justice and rightness about the world. Developed Arians have all the attributes of a winner and are likely to succeed at whatever they put their minds to. Through our many lifetimes with this sign, we develop our leadership, strength, and courage, which are important accomplishments along our evolutionary path.

Taurus

Undeveloped Taureans are stubborn, rigid, and resistant to change. They feel persecuted by any kind of change. Since life *is* change, each passing day challenges them to be more flexible. They are also known for their need for security and love of comfort and the finer things of life. They willingly work long and hard for these things, often indulging afterwards in the sensual pleasures and material rewards of their efforts. Although they are not dull intellectually, their slow, plodding manner, addiction to routine, and lack of openness to the new make them predictable and, sometimes, boring. Undeveloped Taureans may also lack imagination, intuition, vision, and a spiritual perspective.

Although even developed Taureans have some difficulty making changes, their strengths are the undeveloped Taureans' weaknesses honed and refined: stubbornness becomes patience, endurance, and persistence; and their desire for material accomplishment leads to practical contributions to society. With these qualities, they accomplish tasks as a matter of course that other signs find difficult, even insurmountable. Developed Taureans are loyal, steady, hardworking, and reliable, making them the bulwark of society and any organization. We have Taureans to thank for much of the building of our civilization. However, they may still leave the more imaginative tasks to others. Despite this, their love for beauty leads to a refined aesthetic sense, which, if other artistic signs are present, is often reflected in artistic talent. They are connoisseurs of life, who make an art of the sensual pleasures. Developed Taureans also know how to make money. After lifetimes of acquiring wealth and security, providing for their physical needs comes so easily to them that they are often baffled by the struggle others have with this. Through our many Taurean lifetimes, we develop patience, persistence, and determination, which makes it possible for us to create something of value in the world and to provide comfortably for ourselves and others.

Gemini

Geminis are very curious, but the undeveloped Gemini's interest is not easily sustained. They are flighty, unfocused, and superficial. As a result, they are likely to be "a jack-of-all-trades and a master of none," resulting in their accomplishing little of great measure during their early lifetimes. Their mutability creates other problems for them as well. In adapting so easily to their environment and to those around them, they may neglect their own needs and goals. Furthermore, the emphasis on mental exploration in these lifetimes can cause them to live too much in their heads. They may fail to appreciate their bodies, their emotions, and their spirit.

Lifetimes as a Gemini are for tasting the smorgasbord of life. Sampling a variety of life's experiences is their goal—not in-depth appreciation of any one subject. There is a time for everything, as the saying goes. With Gemini, the time is for gathering bits and pieces of information, traveling here and there, and trying out one experience after another. Like a butterfly, they flit from one subject or experience to another, staying only briefly with each. Only after many lifetimes of this have they accumulated enough knowledge to teach. Developed Geminis are teachers. Many lifetimes of querying and seeking develop their mental abilities and facility with language.

The Gemini gift of communication is one of the more valuable gifts. Their ability to put others at ease with their humor and lighthearted banter, and to talk circles around them, results in a charisma few can match. They may or may not be right about what they are saying, but they are able to make themselves heard and respected because of their skillful presentation. Unlike Scorpios, Capricorns, and Leos, they are not trying to influence others through their speech. They are simply expressing themselves and their enjoyment of knowledge. Because their need to learn and communicate is so strong, they spend most of their time reading, listening, writing, and talking with others. Their world is full of communication in one form or another. As a result of pursuing these activities for many lifetimes, they become consummate artists of the spoken and written word. Advanced Geminis bring to the world a lust for knowledge, a keen wit, and a well-refined ability to convey what they have learned as a result of their insatiable curiosity.

Cancer

Cancer is about learning to care for and nurture others, and the best way to learn this is to be cared for lovingly by others. Consequently, the early Cancer lifetimes are ones of dependency. Undeveloped Cancers may experience conditions that prohibit independence, such as illness or retardation. Eventually, they gain some mobility out of this state and, in their next Cancer lifetimes, experience a different kind of dependency. The dependency of these Cancer lifetimes is consciously chosen. It may, for instance, include the experience of being a housewife, a nanny, or a housekeeper. Survival in these situations often hinges on the ability to intuit someone else's feelings and needs. Therefore, they develop a keen sensitivity to the emotions of others. Like the giant's wife in *Jack and the Beanstalk*, they learn to manipulate others to meet their needs and achieve their ends. This lack of power also explains, in part, the moodiness for which they are known. Sacrificing their needs and martyring themselves to others makes them crabby. Furthermore, residual feelings of helplessness from former lifetimes continue to influence how they see themselves and feed their dependency. They need to develop a sense of self and a personal identity separate from others so that they don't feel panicky and empty when a relationship is withdrawn or not available to them.

Cancer's strengths evolve from these early experiences of dependency. As a result, they know what others need, and they have the compassion to respond lovingly to them. These qualities make them ideally suited to caring for others, which is what they do in their later Cancer lifetimes. When they have evolved beyond dependency, many commit their time and energy to creating a family. By preparing delicious meals, decorating the home, providing an understanding ear, or by simply being warm and loving, they build family relationships. Others may nurture those outside the family in professions such as nursing or teaching, or perhaps by running a bed and breakfast. In ministering to others, they find the sense of belonging that they need. Whatever their work, it must give them emotional satisfaction and a feeling of being needed. If it doesn't, they will feel martyred and resentful. Even developed Cancers can be moody, sullen, and crabby if their situation doesn't meet their emotional needs. To be happy, they need to find a niche that provides them with the same warmth and caring that they give to others.

Leo

Undeveloped Leos are playful and fun-loving, but self-centered and oblivious to the needs of others. They are not incapable of understanding others; they just don't bother to try at this stage in their evolution. They are narcissistic—enthralled and enamored with themselves and their abilities. Maybe this is necessary. If it were otherwise, they might not invest time and energy in self-development and self-expression. This, after all, is what this sign is all about. Out of preoccupation with themselves and the desire for attention and power, they seek the spotlight. Once in the spotlight, they must perform! Thus, slowly, over many lifetimes with this sign, their creative and expressive talents develop. The drive to perform and express themselves is all part of the plan of self-development and, more specifically, ego development. They are developing their egos, which is an integral part of our evolution. Lifetimes as a Leo are for doing just that—developing the self as separate and distinct. Unfortunately, their need for power, self-advancement, attention, and superiority interfere with their ability to relate to others as equals.

The strengths of this sign evolve from early egocentricity. Leos' most outstanding quality is their ability to attract and lead followers. The causes over which they unite people may vary dramatically, however, making Leos very different from each other. Nevertheless, the common denominator is their love for being in command and their ability to command the respect they so desire. What is it that makes them charismatic? For one, they have an intense dedication and belief in themselves, which spills over to others. They win the hearts of others with their confidence, optimism, warmth, playfulness, and genuine caring. It's hard to dislike them, no matter how taken they are with themselves. Their huge capacity for enjoying life is contagious, and others hope to catch it. So, with a little bit of a plan, even the least clever of them can win the help they need to accomplish great deeds, though their inspired followers are often the ones who do most of the work.

Their need to instigate and create takes many forms. They may create children, art, pottery, musical compositions, movies, military strategies, inventions, buildings, and more. However, they may not be creative in an artistic sense unless the element of water is also strong. The persistence of this sign enables them to develop talents over their many lifetimes. They make particularly good actors, but their talents don't stop there. They are fine performers of all kinds: musicians, singers, dancers, and comedians. Anything that demands an audience will draw out their talents. In their later lifetimes, they often use the skills they have acquired by creating and performing to lead others. Thus, developed Leos are capable of fine talent and leadership of the highest sort.

They also make excellent teachers. Their love for the limelight, attention, authority, and leadership attracts many of them to this profession. Their expressiveness and drama make them interesting—even spellbinding—speakers. Finally, their own childlike warmth and playfulness make them appealing to children. For all these reasons, they often find their way into professions related to children.

Virgo

Early lifetimes as a Virgo are spent in servile roles. For many reasons, this is valuable to our evolution. For one, servitude provides experience with handling the material exigencies of life. Second, it provides opportunities to develop virtues such as humility, efficiency, thoroughness, and a sense of duty. The drawback to many lifetimes of servitude is that Virgos may fail to develop their own talents. They may give themselves away to others, not for the same reason that Cancers do, but for what they consider to be a higher purpose: service. If they have no fire or other identity-strengthening factors in their chart, they may lose themselves in service to others and wind up bitter and depressed.

In many lifetimes of service, one develops virtues more than skills. The outstanding virtue is dedication to service, which comes from the satisfaction of efficiently carrying out one's responsibilities. Service is the lesson that is learned so well by the time we have lived many lifetimes as a Virgo. Another virtue of the developed Virgo is humility. After learning to transcend the resentment and anger of their first lifetimes of servitude, they become consummate and humble servants. How do they make this leap from resentment to humility? At some point in their evolution, they realize that only goodwill and good work can raise them from their position of servitude, not anger and resentment. By doing good work, they experience their intrinsic worth. By observing the sometimes-frivolous world of the rich, they come to realize that no one is better or worse because of his or her social position or role. Humility comes out of the realization that no one is superior to anyone else. This is what servitude eventually teaches them.

Developed Virgos are dedicated workers, capable of carrying out orders and instructions with pleasure and gratitude for the opportunity to serve; but because they avoid the limelight and work behind the scenes, they rarely get the credit they deserve. Nevertheless, their accomplishments are not dim. Like Taureans, they perform the bulk of the work of society and are its mainstays.

Libra

Libras are very attached to others. They are apt to give their all to the significant people in their lives, sometimes at the expense of their own self-development. They have difficulty making choices and they often allow others to make decisions for them. Dependency is an issue for them, as it is with Cancers. They will come to see that romance needs to be balanced by other things, such as career, friends, and personal goals.

Libras are learning to bring peace and harmony to relationships through cooperation and sharing. A harmonious relationship is an ideal worth working for. Unfortunately, undeveloped Libras often misplace their idealism on their mates, creating gods out of them. This is not beneficial for either person. However, it delivers some important lessons. By doing this, they are challenged to learn to see others clearly and to stop abdicating their power. The combination of dependency and idealization creates the trap. Libras want to believe—and do believe—that their beloved is perfect. If this is true, it removes much of the responsibility of living from their own shoulders, an agreeable situation for those who lean toward dependency. Thus, they find someone who is willing to play the "prince" (or "princess") so that their fantasies can be lived out and confrontation with their own identity avoided. It is an easy way out—or is it? Eventually, the fantasy fades, reality rears its ugly head, and they are left with a shattered dream. What they do then depends on their level of development, but many keep looking for the perfect love. This can continue indefinitely or end in the cold realization that they are ultimately alone in life and must make their own choices. Sometimes this realization is not achieved and integrated until after many lifetimes under this sign. However, Libra's lessons usually need fewer lifetimes in general, perhaps because they can be so painful. Nevertheless, idealization continues to some degree even in the most developed Libras.

What talents develop from this pain? Libras develop peacemaking skills during their many lifetimes in close partnership, and, in later lifetimes, apply them to negotiating, counseling, and mediating. When Libras are developed, they apply their skills to their work as well as to their relationships. Service is the goal of Libran lifetimes, as it is of all lifetimes. Libras are not learning about relationships just for themselves, but to be able to share what they have learned with others. Developed Libras are amicable, friendly, fair, tolerant, and the most advanced in social skills of all the signs. They are pleasing to others without seeking only to please, cooperative and giving without giving themselves away, and tolerant of other points of view while having one of their own. Finally, they are their own person, capable of using their talents to support themselves in the world.

Scorpio

Scorpio is the most maligned of signs. At their worst, Scorpios can be ruthless, vengeful, tenacious, and hard-hitting. Because they are stubborn and determined to have life their way, power struggles are common. This is particularly true in personal relationships, which are very important to them. Undeveloped Scorpios submerge themselves in those they love and attempt to control and manipulate them to their own ends. They are learning to be equal partners, to be intimate, to trust, and to let go of loved ones. These lessons can be difficult. They ask us to be vulnerable to those who may betray us. For undeveloped Scorpios, betrayal is not easily forgiven nor trust easily regained. When a relationship fails, they have difficulty forgiving and moving on emotionally. Their tendency is to blame, find fault, and seek revenge. How is it, then, that they evolve into the powerful, masterful individuals that they are when this sign is developed?

Those who have lived many Scorpio lifetimes have experienced many losses. When we lose someone we love, we have a choice about how we respond. Some responses only create more pain. Scorpios eventually learn that resentment and blame do not heal their broken heart. Eventually, they develop inner strength and a philosophy of life that helps them cope with their pain. They learn how to stand on their own and go on. As a result of their experiences with love and loss, they also develop insight into human nature and life's mysteries. When we lose someone we love, we try to understand why. If it was due to a loved one leaving, we want to know why it didn't work out. If it was the result of death, we want to know why he or she had to die. What is death? Is there a God? Scorpios seek answers to these questions and their trials eventually blossom into strengths.

In their earlier incarnations, Scorpios want to understand life to be better able to control it. They soon find out that life is both uncontrollable and unpredictable. They eventually learn that although they cannot control what life brings them, they can control their responses to it. Instead of trying to control life, they learn to master themselves by mastering their attitudes. This gives them a sense of personal power and conviction. Scorpios know what they believe and they act on the basis of their convictions. Their earlier stubbornness and rigidity are transformed into conviction in their later lifetimes, which they use to help transform others. Scorpios' power is put to better use as they develop because their ideas are now worthy of the force they put behind them. This is what makes them so effective in their later lifetimes. They have the ability to influence people and the refined philosophy that, in itself, can change people's attitudes and their lives. This wisdom is their gift to the world.

Sagittarius

Sagittarians are like Geminis in many respects. Their paths and lessons are very similar. The goal of each is knowledge and understanding, and both are friendly and carefree. The main difference is in the kind of information they seek. Sagittarians compile understanding and philosophy, while Geminis gather facts. The Gemini's subject matter may or may not relate to philosophy, religion, or the law, but these are certain to be the Sagittarian's topics of investigation. The philosophy that Sagittarians adopt depends on their level of development. Advanced Sagittarians hold more metaphysical beliefs, while those less advanced are likely to be more traditional.

Sagittarians are characterized by restless seeking, love of freedom, and wanderlust. These traits take them from place to place or from book to book in search of understanding. As they evolve, their seeking usually takes the form of more study and less travel. In any case, freedom is necessary to their search. However, since freedom is often incompatible with the ordinary demands of life—making a living, preparing food, taking care of others—they may fail to learn to manage these kinds of responsibilities. Yet, this is not true of developed Sagittarians because of their experience under other signs, notably the earth signs. Many lifetimes spent in free exploration and independent activity may also interfere with developing relationship skills. Sagittarians lack sensitivity. They need to become more aware of and responsive to the feelings of others. Eventually, through experiences with the water signs, they do develop more skill with relationships. Because their early explorations often lack direction and purpose, they may also need to learn to set goals and delay gratification. Nevertheless, their early explorations teach them things about life that they couldn't have learned if they had stayed in one place and attended to more mundane concerns.

Developed Sagittarians are wise as a result of their many adventures. By their later lifetimes, the wanderlust of the earlier lifetimes has ripened into a rich appreciation of life. By then, they have moved beyond divisive philosophies to a broader, all-inclusive philosophy, which views life and humanity benevolently. Through their many experiences, they have tasted of the diversity of life and come to understand the underlying principles behind that diversity. This broad understanding is the gift of those born under this sign.

Capricorn

Capricorn is one of the most unpleasant signs in its undeveloped state. Undeveloped Capricorns tend to be greedy and selfish. The selfishness underlying this sign is not the insensitivity and egocentricity of the fire signs, but a true disregard for others. Undeveloped Capricorns are known for their cool approach to emotional matters and relationships, and for their obsession with work. They live to work, stopping at nothing to achieve money, power, status, and recognition. Everything else places a distant second. Relationships may suffer because of this, leaving them alone and empty emotionally.

Capricorns are developing responsibility, reliability, practicality, patience, and endurance, which many of them acquire from lifetimes of literally attending to business. They are also learning to handle authority and power, and must face all the ethical issues involved in that. Even undeveloped Capricorns are driven to work and establish themselves as viable members of society. However, their interest in relationships is minimal. Consequently, those who have lived many lifetimes as a Capricorn and few in signs such as Libra and Cancer may be lacking in compassion and the ability to maintain relationships and nurture others.

Developed Capricorns have much to offer the world. They have the ability to provide for themselves and others, and a remarkable capacity for hard work and practical accomplishment. Because they desire structure, they develop systems, organizations, conventions, and formulas that help society run more smoothly. They build both the social structures and the actual structures. They are socially well adjusted and perform their social and occupational roles as expected. In later lifetimes, their earlier desire for gold and prestige fades, which allows them to invest their practical skills in furthering less self-centered ambitions. Once developed Capricorns have climbed the corporate ladder, they often use their elevated social positions to make changes that will improve society. They become philanthropists or use their skills to help people in other ways.

Aquarius

Aquarians are inventive and creative. They live in a world of ideas. However, because of this, they may miss the experience of communing with life and others in ways other than intellectually. At their best, they are humanitarians or scientific and mathematical geniuses. At their worst, they are emotionally detached, eccentric, or rebellious. Despite their detachment, their friendliness and acceptance of others allows them to get along with many different kinds of people and in all kinds of social situations.

The lessons of Aquarius are not particularly difficult. They pertain to getting along with others, working with others toward mutual goals, subordinating oneself to the group or for the greater good, and bringing forth new ideas to improve society. During their early lifetimes, they get practice working with others, which prepares them for serving within groups in later incarnations.

The one complication on the Aquarian's path is intimate relationships. They do not shine at close range. Their involvement in groups, their desire to serve humanity, and their frequent inhabitation of the mental plane doesn't leave them much time or energy for intimate relationships or the emotional side of life. Their intimate companions, especially those with a strong need for nurturing and closeness, often find them lacking in feeling, difficult to know, and nearly impossible to understand. Their partners are more bothered by this than they are, however. The most likely matches for them are others who have the same need for distance and freedom. However, these kinds of relationships do not help them acquire the skills for forming more satisfying intimate relationships. It will take numerous lifetimes as a Libra, Cancer, or Scorpio to develop the skills they lack.

What is the advantage of this distance? With the other signs, we have seen that some of their weaknesses develop into virtues or gifts. One advantage of the detachment of Aquarius is that it allows them time to develop their unique perspective. Because they don't feel compelled to invest themselves in family life and intimate relationships, they are free to put their energy into other things, such as social and scientific improvements. Another advantage to their detachment is that it fosters tolerance. Their tolerance of others is unsurpassed by any other sign. This may be because their own independence and self-sufficiency allows them to be unattached to how others think and behave.

Aquarians are often found in the social services field or within political organizations. However, they are primarily interested in ideas that will improve the human condition, not in ministering to the masses like Mother Theresa, who was a Virgo. Nevertheless, they see others as intrinsically valuable and worthy of their attention. They have an important role in representing progressive ideals and introducing new ideas that pave the way for future progress and improvement of the human condition.

Pisces

The most evolved Pisceans are highly developed spiritually. The sign represents transcendence and communion with the Divine. However, because transcendence is not possible until a soul is advanced, a degree of spiritual development is necessary before this sign can be expressed in its highest form.

Undeveloped Pisceans have difficulty accepting and dealing with reality. Life is a deep disappointment and a rude joke to many under this sign, leaving them deeply sad and depressed. Many express their drive for transcendence by trying to escape life, most commonly through drugs, alcohol, mental illness, or isolation. Which escape they choose depends mostly on environmental influences. A Piscean child whose parent drinks will be prone to drinking to escape. One whose parent is mentally ill or withdrawn is likely to take one of those routes. Whatever the choice, the goal is to escape the pain and responsibilities of living, which, at times, seem unbearable to them.

Their dreamy nature and gift for imagery predispose them to inner journeying, as do their sensitivity and escapism. They need to acknowledge their sensitivity, learn to value their visions without getting lost in them, and channel their creativity and intuition constructively. As those with this sign evolve, their attunement to other worlds can be put to good use. However, first they must stop running from their fears and accept the responsibilities of being alive. As they evolve, so does their ability to cope with life. They learn practical skills by spending many lifetimes under other signs, particularly the earth signs. Once some ability to deal with reality is developed, they can begin to turn their inner realities outward for all to see. Their ability to visualize can be used to produce lovely paintings; their imagery, to produce poetry; their sensitivity, to produce music; and their empathy and compassion, for healing emotional wounds.

Pisceans are here to serve. The suffering and dependency of their early lifetimes develops their compassion and empathy, which fuel their goal of service in their later lifetimes. By being dependent, both Cancers and Pisceans learn compassion, but the scope of their nurturing is different. In their later lifetimes, Pisceans extend love to the entire world, not just to family members, and it includes healing by sharing their spiritual vision. Through service, they heal their sense of loneliness and alienation. Their feeling of not belonging in the world is remedied by knowing that they belong to another world—the world of the spirit—and by their ability to serve others by translating this realm for them. Pisceans at this level are often psychics or mediums. Once the earlier lessons are learned, their attunement to the world beyond the senses finally has a place. At their most advanced, they are religious leaders and spiritual teachers who guide others in understanding the Self and the nature of the universe. They are the mystics and the gurus who heal not only the psyche but also the soul.

Some Lessons Take Longer to Learn

The lessons of some signs take more lifetimes to learn than others. For example, a degree of spiritual development must be reached before the full range of Piscean lessons can be taught. The intuition and psychic abilities for which Pisces is known take many lifetimes to develop and don't begin developing until our later incarnations. Many of the Piscean lessons cannot be encountered until these abilities are developed.

The lessons of Aries may take more lifetimes to learn than other signs, too. Learning patience is easy enough, but learning courage can take a long time if someone has become fearful. When risk-taking has led to disaster, it may take many lifetimes to move beyond the fear. Many lifetimes may be spent choosing Aries in an attempt to break through the fear left over from just one traumatic experience.

Another sign that is chosen more frequently than others is Gemini. Because of the mind's complexity and the enormous task it has in processing information, many lifetimes as a Gemini are needed to develop its capabilities. There is no end to the amount of intelligence we can develop. Some choose Gemini repeatedly as a way of developing either a creative, intuitive mind (chosen with water signs) or a more logical, scientific one.

Choosing Our Chart

Although we do not experience the signs in any set order, the choice of signs is purposeful. The signs are chosen in keeping with the lessons we need and with our individual preferences. The first priority is balancing our karmic debts. Signs are chosen to do this and, at the same time, teach one or more of the basic lessons. Once some of our basic lessons are mastered, we are given more freedom to choose our charts. At this stage, the part of our consciousness that remains after death collaborates with our soul in choosing our chart. So, eventually, we are allowed to choose signs to accomplish whatever we want. Each of us is unique, and we evolve uniquely as well. Sometimes we have trouble with a sign and have to repeat a grade, so to speak, while we speed through the lessons of other signs. Although we all need to experience every lesson of the twelve signs, how we do this and how long it takes is individual and a matter of choice, particularly as the soul progresses.

Our free will is hardly inconsequential to our evolution. If evolution were only about learning certain lessons, we could all do this in approximately the same way. However, the purpose of life—the Creator's intent, if I can be so presumptuous—is to experience all possibilities and to evolve from this infinite diversity. How else can this be done except through free will, which allows us to explore all possibilities? A Plan is chosen and our free will operates within that Plan. This is how human evolution and the evolution of the godhead is carried out. When we choose a chart, we choose it to learn lessons, develop talents, and fulfill a life task, but also because we have a desire to experience life through certain signs. Where does this desire come from? Why do we have certain preferences?

THE SEVEN ROLES

Why we each have our own preferences of signs is not such a mystery if we understand that we are sent from the godhead with general inclinations and goals. I am referring to what some call "Roles." Before its set of physical incarnations, each soul takes on a Role that pertains to a goal for all its physical incarnations. The incarnations and the life tasks, in particular, relate to this Role.

Each Role favors certain signs because some signs suit the Role's task and its way of being. There are seven Roles, thus, seven goals, each exhibiting its own style and each favoring certain signs. This helps explain why some signs in a chart may be more advanced than others: they have been chosen more often because the person's Role favors them. Those who are advanced enough to have the freedom to choose their charts usually express their Roles in the charts they pick. Thus, the Role can often be surmised from the chart. However, sometimes a chart is chosen to balance the characteristics of a Role.

There are seven Roles: Priest, Servant (Slave), King, Warrior, Scholar, Artisan, and Sage. Chelsea Quinn Yarbro first presented this concept in her book *Messages from Michael*.

Priest

When allowed to, Priests choose incarnations that enable them to explore the unconscious and the emotions. They are interested in religions of all kinds, meditation, psychology, dreams, psychic phenomena, and other areas that take them beyond the five senses and the material world. Because of their drive to explore other realms, some find themselves in trouble with drugs and alcohol, but usually only in their early incarnations. They eventually share the insight and understanding that they gain in their explorations with others as spiritual leaders, healers, counselors, ministers, and teachers. They are rarely found in subservient positions, since these do not provide the freedom to pursue the understanding and wisdom they crave.

Pisces is a favorite sign, but only in conjunction with the fire signs, which help Priests develop the leadership skills they need to act as spiritual guides or teachers. Sagittarius is their other favorite sign. Leo and Aries are frequently chosen as well, but only to aid their search for understanding and the acquisition of spiritual strength and leadership, not for gaining power in a material or mundane sense. Virgo is not a favorite sign, nor is it particularly needed. A lack of humility is not usually a problem with this Role, since the ego's desires don't hold as much sway for Priests as they do for the other Roles.

As for the elements, Priests' charts are most often composed of fire and water signs, some air, and little earth. Occasionally, these charts contain earth to help Priests acquire the following that they need. For the most part, Priests gain their following because of their spiritual power and not because of material success.

Besides an abundance of fire and water, another clue to identifying this Role is in the Moon's nodes. The nodes are most often in Gemini/Sagittarius, although Leo/Aquarius is common, too. Since the life task and Role are often related, analyzing the nodes is helpful in identifying the Role.

The life tasks for this Role can take many forms and usually pertain to providing spiritual guidance and understanding.

Depending on the culture, this may mean psychological guidance or even medical guidance, as with shamans. Although some people who perform these functions have little traditional training, all but the most undeveloped Priests involve themselves in stringent mental and spiritual disciplines to attain the caliber of understanding required of them. Consequently, the air signs are important in acquiring the educational training and social skills they need to fulfill their tasks.

Of the air signs, Libra and Gemini are most frequently chosen. Libra provides counseling skill, while Gemini supplies the curiosity and motivation to learn what is needed to be a spiritual teacher. Aquarius is chosen least because it doesn't allow them the leadership and authority they enjoy. Priests give comfort and healing to those they serve, but they are not one of them.

Scorpio is the water sign most favored by Priests, after Pisces. Cancer is chosen the least. The dependency, emotional involvement, and responsibilities entailed in family life do not foster leadership skills nor allow them enough freedom. Likewise, Scorpio is not as ideal as Pisces. Yet the lessons pertaining to dependency, intimacy, and relationship cannot be entirely avoided even by Priests.

The earth sign most favored is Capricorn because it fosters leadership and initiative. Taurus and Virgo, on the other hand, are two of the least chosen signs. These signs rarely aid the Priest's work, and their lessons are not particularly difficult for them to master.

The other fire signs, Aries and Leo, are helpful and favored as well. Rarely do Priests lack strength in the element of fire, since the life task is likely to need fire. If little fire is present in the Priest's chart, the individual may have developed the fiery gifts so completely in others lifetimes that fire needs to be represented only minimally. Because an element that is totally absent is a clue to characteristics that are not important to the life task, this information should be used in delineating the Role and the life task.

Servant

Servants, also known as Slaves, have a goal of service, too. However, their service is not limited to serving the spiritual needs of others as it is with Priests. In early incarnations, their service is likely to entail menial duties and subservient roles, which teach them to love service for service's sake. In later incarnations, after they have learned to serve humbly and happily, they serve by choice and may even become famous for their selfless acts. They never seek notoriety, however, unless it helps their life task by allowing them to reach more people.

Virgo, Pisces, Cancer, and Libra are common in Servants' charts. Their charts usually have both earth and water signs. The earth signs afford them the practical know-how and determination to dedicate themselves to helping others. If their service depends on mental activity, air signs will be highlighted as well. Because water signs develop the compassion, love, and kindness so necessary to service, they are the cornerstones of this Role.

It is rare for Servants not to have water in their charts. If it becomes necessary for a Servant to balance an overly watery nature by eliminating water signs from the chart for a while, the qualities of water will still be apparent in the personality. When a balancing life is chosen, it is usually to gain more self-confidence and independence, for which the fire signs are useful. Otherwise, fire signs are not helpful to them.

The Servant's Moon's nodes are most often in Pisces/Virgo, but Cancer/Capricorn is fairly common as well. The Pisces/Virgo axis represents service, and these are their two favorite signs. However, Cancer/Capricorn nodes also allow them to serve others, particularly family members. When the North Node is in Capricorn, which is rare, it is usually to balance overly dependent and self-sacrificing behavior. Giving too much of ourselves to others is not service, but dishonoring ourselves. This is one of their major lessons, which even advanced Servants may struggle with. Shifting the North Node from Cancer to Capricorn and adding fire signs to the chart are the methods most often used to overcome this tendency.

King

Kings have life tasks that involve leadership and enterprise. Their goal is self-expression and the advancement of new projects or ideas. Their accomplishments are varied, but the experience of leadership underlies them all. Their charts are chosen to develop self-confidence, self-assertion, proper use of power, organizational ability, foresight, and understanding, all qualities necessary for good leadership. Over the course of their lifetimes, Kings learn that good leaders promote what is best for the majority, and they develop the foresight to know what that is.

Kings are fiery and cardinal, and they choose charts that reflect these qualities. The cardinal signs most suited to them are Capricorn and Aries. They also favor Leo and Sagittarius.

Unless they find themselves leading in intellectual spheres, air is not likely to be prominent in their charts. This is true even though intelligence, education, and diplomacy are important in most leadership tasks. When diplomacy is important, Libra is chosen.

Earth signs, however, are likely. Earth signs give the practical know-how, logic, and realistic approach that form the basis of sound judgment. The earth signs, especially Capricorn, give the determination and desire for power and prestige, which stimulate the development of traits needed for strong leadership. The King's least favorite signs are Cancer, Libra, Pisces, and Virgo. Sometimes Kings have to choose these signs for a few lifetimes to learn to share power, to develop compassion, or to learn humility or other basic lessons. They may have difficulty with humility in particular. It is easy for them to assume that they are superior when they attract power so easily. The lesson of humility is their biggest challenge, one they may not entirely master, even in their later lifetimes.

The King's North Node is likely to be in Leo or Capricorn, occasionally in Aries, and less frequently in Taurus, though a Taurus placement is favorable for the King because of its ability to accumulate wealth, which gives Kings power in most societies. Taurus also supplies the persistence and determination needed to accomplish great deeds. When the North Node is in Aries, it usually symbolizes the need to develop ego strength before being ready to lead. This is more of a preparatory placement for Kings than one chosen in later lifetimes, when they are actually in positions of authority. In later lifetimes, the North Node is often in Leo or Capricorn. However, if their life task involves spiritual leadership, for instance, the North Node may be in Pisces. Obviously, the particular life task influences the nodal placement.

Warrior

Because Warriors and Kings are alike in their goals and styles, they choose similar charts. However, the Warrior's purpose is not leadership but conquest and exploration. For them, leadership is merely a means to an end. Both Kings and Warriors are dynamic, assertive, confident, courageous, and unrelenting. Warriors apply these traits to exploration, adventure, and conquest for its own sake. Kings do these things only if they apply to their goal of rulership.

The purpose of the Warrior's many lifetimes is to build strength, courage, stamina, and physical prowess. Their life tasks may involve daring business ventures, athletic achievements, championing the weak, and courageous feats that inspire excellence in others. They stretch the limits of what humankind can accomplish, thus inspiring further achievements and expanding human capacities.

Warriors' charts emphasize fire and deemphasize water. Water does not help them attain their goals, nor do they particularly enjoy lifetimes with the water signs. Water requires involvement with family, friends, and emotional issues, which goes against their restless, independent, and conquering nature. To them, emotions are something to be overcome so that they do not interfere with their goals. Therefore, they spend as little time as possible developing this side of themselves. Instead, they devote themselves to strengthening the traits that will further their goals.

Air is helpful to them because it provides the objectivity and extroversion they need to disengage themselves from the emotional realm and from people whose fear may inhibit their courage. A strong Uranus, characteristic of Warriors, is often chosen to enhance their daring and adventuresome spirit.

Earth is not often found in Warriors' charts except in their early lifetimes, when it provides the common sense and stability needed for good judgment and the physical skills needed for their later life tasks. Once enough lifetimes have been spent with the earth signs, Warriors avoid them. Earth signs provide too much caution and practicality, which can interfere with their achieving their superhuman goals. Nevertheless, sometimes earth is just what they need to balance their overly zealous nature and sense of invincibility, and to keep them from overstepping the bounds of good judgment.

Scholar

Scholars contribute to society intellectually by analyzing and compiling existing information. They are key to the maintenance of civilization, but generally are not involved in the creation of new ideas. Their life tasks usually involve research, teaching, writing, lecturing, reporting, establishing and maintaining libraries, editing, publishing, and scholarly studies. Their contributions are likely to be in the form of ideas, plans, abstractions, analysis, observations, comparisons, and statistics.

Air is likely to be the strongest element in their charts, with earth being the second. Air gives them the ability and desire to explore the realm of ideas objectively and analytically, while earth gives them the patience and persistence to pursue their intellectual endeavors. Scholars enjoy the exchange of ideas, whether or not they personally support those ideas. They rarely become involved in causes because that would detract from their goal of compiling and analyzing data. For the same reason, they choose water signs as infrequently as possible, relying on others to provide the emotional element in their lives. Although this can be frustrating for their partners, who may not get their emotional needs met, emotional people gain objectivity through their relationships with Scholars, which may be the purpose of such a relationship.

Because fire is not particularly necessary or helpful to Scholars, it is not usually chosen except to balance their overly intellectual approach with physical activity. Fire would add restlessness and impatience to their personality, which might interfere with their need to persist during the dry, unexciting moments so common to intellectual pursuits.

Virgo is a favorite sign, along with Gemini and Aquarius. Virgo provides the mental discipline and attention to detail that their work requires. Capricorn and Taurus are helpful as well, supplying the drive to accomplish something for society and the ability to wade through endless piles of information. Because its sociability outweighs its intellectuality, Libra chosen too frequently is likely to interfere with their work, which mostly takes place in isolation.

Their North Node is often in Gemini or Aquarius, and less frequently in Libra. When it is in Gemini, it is likely to indicate a lifetime of study, teaching, writing, speaking, or accumulating data. In Aquarius, the North Node is likely to indicate a life task involving a team or scientific research or both. The North Node in Libra might mean that a partnership is significant to the life task. The Scholar's North Node is not found in Virgo as often as you might think because this nodal axis is most common to life tasks involving healing or service.

Artisan

The Artisan's goal is creativity and self-expression. Their creations take many forms: art, music, dance, poetry, pottery, crafts, decorating, design, fashion, jewelry, and anything else that incorporates a new, fresh approach or style. The Artisan's urge to create comes from deep within and does not let them rest until it has been expressed. They see life through different eyes than most and catch subtleties that others without their keen sensitivities miss. Their fresh viewpoint, which they bring to others through their creations, renews us. Their work could be considered spiritual, for their creations reflect the transcendent and sublime aspect of life. Thus, they have an important mission, though it is not always recognized as such.

Artisans usually have charts strong in water and fire, the creative elements. Water provides the sensitivity to capture creative inspirations from the unconscious realm and beyond, and fire provides the drive to express them. Earth is needed in their early lifetimes to develop the skills and discipline needed to materialize their creations. However, later on it is likely to add too much practicality and conventionality to be useful. Whether or not air is present depends on what form the creativity takes. It will be present if the creations call for it, as they do in creative writing or poetry; otherwise, it may not.

Any placement of the Moon's nodes is possible with Artisans. However, the North Node in Cancer, Pisces, Virgo, Taurus, Leo, or Libra is more likely than other placements. These are also their favorite signs. Taurus and Libra, because Venus rules them, are favored, as is Virgo for its craftsmanship and attention to detail, and Leo for its urge to create.

Sage

Sages seek both wisdom and self-expression. Because they are after truth and wisdom, they involve themselves in study—not in the way Scholars do—but in the study of life itself, with themselves as the main subject. One way they do this is through acting. The stage is a place where they can try out the various characters, experiences, and emotions they come across in their explorations. It allows them to examine the nuances of the emotions and the human condition without *living* the emotions, which would not suit their style or their goals.

Fire and air signs, especially Gemini and Sagittarius, are most suited to them because Sages require the freedom to explore their environment and themselves independent of the needs of others. Fire and air signs are useful because they help them to observe life freshly and objectively. Leo is a favorite sign, too. It encourages them to explore their creativity and expressive potential, which is another way they come to understand themselves and others. Aquarius is also favored because its independent, tolerant, and progressive outlook suits their goals. However, Aquarius' group orientation does not appeal to them.

Sages invest little time in exploring relationships and the emotional side of life because they need freedom to accomplish their goals. They leave this side of life to others, except as it relates to their goals. Nevertheless, they frequently choose Scorpio because it allows them to study others and themselves. However, the side of Scorpio that becomes entangled in relationships is not for them. Once they have learned the watery lessons, they usually stay away from the water signs, though they may continue to choose Scorpio to hone their psychological understanding.

Occasionally, Sages choose earth signs to foster stability and responsibility. They need to learn to handle everyday responsibilities. This is usually accomplished in early lifetimes so that later they can devote themselves to their explorations.

The Sage's North Node is most frequently in Sagittarius or Gemini, sometimes in Scorpio, and less frequently in Aquarius or Leo. Their life tasks are likely to involve teaching, speaking, writing, or drama.

UNCOVERING WHY A PARTICULAR CHART IS CHOSEN

If our chart is very different from our Role, it won't feel natural. A Warrior, for instance, would feel frustrated with a watery chart, but the chart would deliver some important lessons. The usual reason for choosing a chart that doesn't suit our Role is to balance the negative tendencies of a certain sign, which may have become ingrained by choosing that sign repeatedly over many lifetimes.

There are ways of identifying why a particular chart was chosen. The clues to this lie in the themes, the Moon's nodes, and Saturn. When the South Node's sign is very different from the predominant signs in the chart, the chart may have been chosen to balance the negative tendencies of the South Nodes' sign. Because Saturn in a sign indicates the tendency to display too much of the negative or too little of the positive qualities of that sign, Saturn in one of the predominant signs or in one very different from the predominant themes also points to the likelihood that this is a balancing lifetime. The following example illustrates this.

This King was born with a Pisces Sun, Cancer Moon, and Saturn and the North Node in Cancer. Although in previous lifetimes, he developed courage, self-confidence, and charisma, he became autocratic and lacked the ability to lead kindly and compassionately. To learn sensitivity, this watery chart was chosen, which contained signs relatively unfamiliar to him.

Because of his former strengths, he is naturally inclined toward leadership. However, in this lifetime, he has not been given opportunities to lead. Rather, he is being asked to serve and care for others. If he tries to lead, he will be steered back toward service. With his Sun and Moon both in water signs, he is being encouraged to focus on emotions and personal relationships; because he is unfamiliar with these signs, he sometimes appears less evolved than he is.

The need to learn compassion and fairness is represented by his nodes and by Saturn in Cancer. Saturn and the North Node in Cancer in the eleventh house indicate the importance of learning to nurture others and the need to apply that toward the greater good as part of a group rather than as its leader. The South Node in Capricorn in the fifth house indicates his having been overly absorbed in career and leadership in the past.

Knowing why a chart is chosen is important in interpreting it. In our earlier incarnations, we choose charts to learn lessons that are basic to evolution. We choose charts with each of the twelve signs until we have attained a degree of mastery of each sign. While we learn the lessons of the signs, we develop the talents of these signs. Once we are beyond the basic evolutionary lessons, there are two reasons for choosing a chart, besides balancing our karma: we choose signs we favor, or we choose signs to balance too many lifetimes with our favorite sign(s). If the latter is the case, that life will be focused on learning the lessons of the less familiar signs. If the former is the case, we will be enhancing the skills and talents of our favorite signs and applying them to our life task.

To summarize, there are four reasons for choosing the signs in the chart:

1. to balance karma;

2. to balance negative tendencies from former lifetimes;

3. to learn the basic lessons of the signs;

4. to further develop and use the talents of the signs.

How do you determine which possibility is true for a chart? We have already seen how to analyze the chart for karma. As for the second point, comparing the information from Saturn, the Moon's nodes, and the themes should reveal if the chart's purpose is to balance negative tendencies. The key question for the last two possibilities is: How skillfully are the prominent signs being expressed? If the answer is "not very," then the chart may have been chosen to learn the basic lessons of those signs. If the answer is "quite skillfully" or "very skillfully," then the chart is likely to have been chosen to further develop or use the talents of the signs.

It might be helpful to note that people still working on the basic lessons at the most elementary level rarely seek out an astrologer. However, this doesn't mean that everyone who goes to an astrologer is expressing the signs in his or her chart positively. People express the signs in their charts negatively for reasons other than their level of development. Immaturity, youth, stress, and emotional wounding are all reasons why people might not be living up to the potential in their charts.

So, the signs in a chart are chosen to develop or use a talent, learn lessons (basic lessons or karmic lessons), or balance negative tendencies. Both the tendencies that need balancing and the talents are likely to relate to the Role. The following lists describe the talents of each Role and the negative tendencies that can result from frequently choosing the Role's favorite signs.

Relationship Between Signs and Roles

The following list summarizes the relationship between the Roles and the signs. It lists the elements and signs most frequently chosen by the Roles.

Priest (water and fire): Pisces, Sagittarius, Scorpio, Leo, and Aries

Servant (water and earth): Pisces, Virgo, Cancer, and Libra

King (fire and cardinal): Leo, Aries, Capricorn, Sagittarius, and Libra

Warrior (fire and Uranus): Aries, Sagittarius, Leo, and Capricorn

Scholar (air and earth): Gemini, Aquarius, and Virgo

Artisan (water and fire): Cancer, Pisces, Leo, Taurus, Libra, and Virgo

Sage (air and fire): Leo, Sagittarius, Gemini, and Aquarius

The Talents of Each Role

Priest: counseling, speaking, spiritual healing, religious leadership

Servant: efficient and thorough service, dedication to a task, humility

King: leadership, political prowess, speaking, executive ability, a flare for drama

Warrior: military expertise, leadership, courage, strength, self-assertion, championing causes

Scholar: academic expertise, writing, speaking, logical analysis, teaching

Artisan: creative inspiration and expression, artistic talent, craftsmanship, manual and physical dexterity

Sage: wisdom, cultural erudition, acting, speaking, teaching

Tendencies That May Need Balancing

Priest: too much introspection; needs to develop relationship skills

Servant: lack of identity and self-esteem; needs to develop an identity, confidence, and assertiveness

King: lack of compassion and sensitivity to others; needs to develop compassion, empathy, and equality in relationships

Warrior: lack of compassion and sensitivity to others; needs to develop compassion, empathy, and cooperation

Scholar: lack of common sense and practical know-how; needs to be involved in the ordinary aspects of life, especially in practical tasks and relationships

Artisan: lack of skill with relationships and dealing with the world; needs to learn social skills and conformity

Sage: lack of practical expertise; needs to develop practical skills and be involved in service and in the ordinary aspects of life

EVOLUTION AND THE ELEMENTS

The elements play an important role in evolution. Earth and water preserve and maintain the status quo, fire strengthens our vision and capabilities, and air expands our mental abilities and social skills. Thus, earth and water are basic to human survival, and fire and air expand human potentials.

The lessons of some elements need to be learned before others. Earth is the element most crucial to survival, so its lessons must be learned first. Consequently, earth signs are prominent in the charts of those just beginning their evolutionary journey. Water is the element developed next. It provides the glue that binds social groups, which ensures their survival and advancement. Fire is next, providing the inspiration and energy to seek new ideas and avenues of expression that will expand the boundaries of society. Finally, air develops the intellect, allowing for refinement of social mores and improved technology, which frees people to seek goals beyond survival and maintenance. The elements evolve in this general pattern, with each overlapping the next: earth continues to develop followed by water. Earth and water continue to develop followed by fire. Earth, water, and fire continue to develop followed by air. Please keep in mind that these are generalizations and that you can't determine how evolved someone is by the signs in his or her chart. Older souls choose earth signs too, but for different reasons than younger souls do.

The names I have used for the stages of evolution are the ones used in *Messages from Michael* by Chelsea Quinn Yarbro. However, for simplicity, I have included the Infant stage in the description of the Baby stage rather than addressing it separately. There are very few Infant souls on the planet today. Each stage—or cycle—of evolution has its own purpose and way of viewing the world, and its favorite signs or elements. The four cycles are: Baby, Young, Mature, and Old.

THE CYCLES

The Baby Cycle

The Baby cycle is the first cycle. The overriding emotion of this cycle is fear. Baby souls are fearful about everything—and rightfully so. At this point in our evolution, we have little experience with life, few emotional resources and mechanisms for coping, only the most basic intellectual equipment, and little ability to intuit our Plans. The earth signs are chosen during this cycle to provide survival skills and practical life experience. Nevertheless, not having the experience or wisdom of later lifetimes, Baby souls are destined to find out about life the hard way—through trial and error. Because we often make some serious mistakes in this cycle, it is the hardest cycle of all.

Many of the youngest Baby souls live in mental hospitals or prisons because their lack of wisdom and resources gets them into trouble. Those in mental hospitals are there because they have been unable to cope with reality, or because they have chosen this life to learn how to cope. Other Baby souls reside in secluded or rural parts of the world, where they live simply, focused on basic needs and family. Until later in this cycle, Baby souls are rarely found in large cities or in positions that demand complex organization or thought. They don't have the resources to deal with the stress and confusion that these circumstances create for them. When they do find themselves in these circumstances, criminal or antisocial behavior may result.

Later in this cycle, Baby souls develop strong opinions and believe that others should be like them. Because they have difficulty accepting other points of view, they often gather in like-minded groups that support their views and lifestyle. Many join religious and political organizations that try to convert others. They are not empathetic or sensitive to the needs of others, which is one reason for their narrow outlook.

The Young Cycle

By the time we are in the Young cycle, we have gained more objectivity, tolerance, self-control, and ability to function in society. What Young souls do to support themselves depends on their Role and their lessons. During this cycle, as with the Baby cycle, the life task and basic lessons are usually the same. Not until the Mature cycle do life tasks independent of the basic lessons emerge.

Young souls have less fear and more ego-strength than Baby souls. This is the "me cycle." The ego's hold is the strongest in this cycle, and the ego-drives rule. Young souls are on a quest for power, beauty, wealth, and prestige. Getting these things and learning what it means to have them are important lessons of this cycle. The Young cycle is a time for gaining more experience in the world, developing our egos, and exploring many different identities. As a result of this exploration, we are better able to extend sympathy and tolerance to others in the Mature cycle.

The Mature Cycle

In the Mature cycle, we have progressed beyond many of the basic lessons and we begin working on life tasks that pertain to our Role. One of the major tasks of this cycle is developing the intellect more fully. The intellect is exercised and refined by working on our life tasks and by developing our talents, another focus of the Mature cycle. The talents we develop depend on our Role and our preferences formed in previous incarnations.

An outstanding feature of the Mature cycle is its introversion. Mature souls question who they are and search for answers to help them cope with the emptiness and restlessness of this stage. During the Mature cycle, we sense that there is more to life, but we are still unable to consistently experience ourselves as the God-beings that we are. We long for what is just beyond our reach. This longing and searching brings results in the Old cycle. Until then, it often leads Mature souls to the psychiatrist's couch, the guru's lap, or drugs or alcohol to ease their angst. The process of seeking relief from this pain advances our intellects and understanding of human nature.

The Old Cycle

The Old cycle is the last stage in our evolution on the physical plane. During these lifetimes, we are absorbed in our life tasks, which usually relate to service. Any karmic lessons we face are usually ones that could not be balanced earlier for some reason, since few Old souls incur serious karma. Unlike earlier cycles, in the Old cycle occupation is not as important as the quality of life. The goal for this cycle is peace and attunement to higher dimensions. For this, a traditional or highly stressful job may be a hindrance unless it suits the life task. Because of this, Old souls often lead simple lives, close to nature. During the Old cycle, we are able— at last—to experience ourselves as more than our personality, our body, our emotions, or our social position on a more consistent basis. These aspects of ourselves, the ones we strove so hard to strengthen as a younger soul, are put in proper perspective in the Old cycle. Instead, we seek higher understanding, greater love, and unity with all of life.

HOW THE ELEMENTS EVOLVE

Each of the elements plays a particular role in each cycle. What follows is a description of how the elements evolve in each of the cycles and their role in evolution.

Earth

The qualities developed over many lifetimes with this element ensure our survival. Earth signs teach us responsibility, reliability, practicality, realism, perseverance, patience, and caution. Saturn, the ruler of Capricorn, in particular, develops these qualities through its transits to the natal chart. Because these qualities are essential to our survival, the earth signs are the signs chosen most frequently in the Baby cycle, with Capricorn being the first earth sign to be developed.

Capricorn is particularly helpful in the Baby and Young cycles because it arouses distrust, fearfulness, and pessimism, which inspire caution, responsibility, and patience. Because acting cautiously, responsibly, and patiently helps us avoid what we fear, we come to value these qualities. By the Mature and Old cycles, if we have spent many lifetimes as a Capricorn, these qualities are deeply ingrained so that even when Capricorn is not in our chart, these qualities are still available to us. Capricorn, once it is mastered in the early lifetimes, provides us with a secure foundation from which to grow in other ways.

Once we are able to provide for our basic survival, as accomplished through several lifetimes with Capricorn, we continue to enhance our practical skills in the Baby cycle through Taurus lifetimes. In these, we work hard to obtain security and the comforts of life. Unlike Capricorn lifetimes, Taurus lifetimes are not as concerned with status and wealth as with comforts. Our earliest Taurus lifetimes are likely to explore comfortable living and the sensual pleasures of life. By pursuing sensual pleasures during the Baby and Young cycles, we come to realize that they are not the answer to happiness. So, early Taurus lifetimes continue to build our practical skills while serving as beginning lessons about values.

Virgo lifetimes usually follow Taurus lifetimes in the late Baby cycle. During these lifetimes, our practical skills are refined by the intellect and more efficiently applied to our survival needs. Virgo teaches us to plan, organize, and economize. This streamlines the attainment of our material needs, freeing us to satisfy other needs. In this way, Virgo provides another step along the way to becoming more self-sufficient and easily sustained.

The earth signs continue to be important in the Young cycle for their survival value. However, Capricorn plays a slightly different role in the Young cycle than in the Baby cycle by nurturing a budding social awareness. As a result, we begin to function more as members of society. The Young cycle represents the dawning of a social conscience. However, this social conscience is often not developed until we have first broken the law and, consequently, learned respect for the law and convention. In this stage of evolution, Capricorn shows us the importance of law, structure, and self-discipline.

Taurus teaches loyalty, love, and responsibility within the family unit in the late Baby and Young cycles. It focuses our energy on work and productivity for the benefit of our family and ourselves. Late Baby and Young Taureans often live simple lives within small communities from which they draw their sustenance. This is the time in human evolution when the family unit begins to hold real meaning for us, and we feel fiercely loyal to those family bonds.

Virgo is chosen in the late Baby and Young cycles to develop the mind, manual skills, and attention to basic hygiene and health care. At this stage, we are better able to apply our common sense and knowledge to developing specific skills, which allow us to function more efficiently in the world. Late Baby and Young Virgos are likely to develop skills such as blacksmithing, weaving, sewing, basket weaving, shoemaking, pottery, and other crafts as more specialized means of survival. Virgo lifetimes in the late Young cycle enhance our desire to serve, and mark the beginning of the path of service.

Although the importance of the earth signs lessens with soul age, they play a significant—although different—role in the Mature cycle. Capricorn is chosen during the Mature cycle for its ability to contribute to society through enterprising leadership. The skills acquired earlier are applied for the good of society and less for selfish reasons. Capricorns at this level can usually capture positions of prominence and leadership in the social and business world, becoming active citizens who contribute politically and financially to the community.

Taurus is chosen during the Mature cycle to increase our ability to produce something useful for others, something that will raise the standard of living and the degree of comfort for others. Taureans at this level are excellent workers, capable of great accomplishments through perseverance and sheer determination. These can be highly productive lifetimes for Taureans.

Virgo is chosen in the Mature cycle to enhance service and intellectual accomplishment. The efficiency and dedication developed in earlier lifetimes is applied to service in its many forms, especially in the healing professions.

Once we progress to the Old cycle, the need for earth signs diminishes unless they help with our life task. When earth signs are present, they serve the same purposes they did in the Mature cycle.

Water

Water evolves next. Water signs pertain to developing the emotions, particularly those involved in loving others. Each water sign serves a special purpose in the evolution of water's qualities. Cancer develops our ability to nurture and care for others, Scorpio develops our ability to share and be intimate with a partner, and Pisces develops our compassion and love for the broader family of humankind.

Dependency begets love. This is no less true in an evolutionary sense. In our earliest incarnations, love is learned within our first dependent relationships. Through our experiences of being loved and cared for, our ability to love grows. This is the purpose of our earliest Cancer lifetimes. Our ability to love is developed further by Scorpio lifetimes, which explore intimacy and love between equals. Through Scorpio lifetimes, we learn to share equally and lovingly with a partner. The love learned in these lifetimes becomes a model for the nonpersonal love of our Piscean lifetimes, which come later. In this way, personal love and its lessons lay the foundation for unconditional love and altruistic service.

In the Baby cycle, we invariably choose several Cancer lifetimes, but only after several Capricorn lifetimes. Capricorn lifetimes are needed to develop some ego-strength before the dependency of a Cancer lifetime is helpful. Otherwise, dependency may just foster more dependency rather than independence. If we are unable to see ourselves as capable of giving support, only of receiving it, we will not develop the capacity to care for others. Cancer lifetimes complement the earlier Capricorn lifetimes in another way. They involve us in the emotional side of life, which our earlier Capricorn lifetimes neglected because of their focus on self-preservation and self-development.

Scorpio is rarely chosen during the Baby cycle for two reasons: Cancer lifetimes of dependency must precede Scorpio lifetimes, and Scorpio's deep, introspective nature does not suit the Baby cycle. Nevertheless, Scorpio is the water sign most likely to be highlighted in the Young cycle, when the tasks are learning to trust, share, cooperate, and be intimate. Experiences with intimacy as a Scorpio during the Young cycle develop our understanding of human nature. Although both Cancer and Scorpio play an important role in the Baby and Young cycles in teaching us to love, not until the Mature cycle do the deeper, sensitive, and intuitive sides of these two signs emerge.

Pisces is chosen less frequently in our earliest lifetimes than the other water signs. Baby souls need to be practical, and Pisces does not contribute to practicality. Pisces usually enters the picture during the Young cycle, when it is chosen to develop compassion and love through dependency, as in the Cancer lifetimes. Not until the Mature and Old cycles is Pisces chosen for service.

In the Mature cycle, we no longer choose Cancer to experience dependency but to exercise caring for others. By the Mature cycle, the tables are turned, and the compassion developed by being cared for is expressed through compassionate and loving care of others. During the Mature cycle, Cancers extend their care mostly to family members. It may not be until the Old cycle that it is extended to those outside this circle.

Likewise, Scorpios in the Mature cycle are capable of giving to others in intimate relationships in ways not possible before. Young cycle power struggles and jealousies taught them to love. Now, in the Mature cycle, they can form satisfying love relationships. Scorpio is a favorite sign of Mature souls because the Mature cycle is a time of psychological exploration and self-awareness. In the Old cycle, Scorpio is chosen to expand this search for understanding to include the metaphysical.

Pisces is highlighted in the Mature cycle because of this cycle's concern with service and spiritual understanding. Mature souls ask many questions about life and experience more anxiety, depression, and neuroses than those in the earlier cycles. This is probably because their energy is freed from the demands of the basic lessons, including survival. Consequently, growth in the Mature cycle is of an inner, emotional, and spiritual nature. A philosophy is sought and the seeds of a larger understanding are planted. Through service to others during this cycle, Pisceans gain in understanding and love.

Scorpio and Pisces are favored in the Old cycle for building on the love and understanding begun in the Mature cycle. Because love and understanding are the goals of life, Scorpio and Pisces further our spiritual development and complete the purpose for our incarnations.

Fire

The element of fire serves a different purpose than earth or water. Fire is the inspirational element. It motivates, inspires, creates, and transforms. Fire brings into manifestation new insights, new approaches, new outlooks, and new ways of being in the world. With the addition of fire to the evolutionary process, we are able to grow and expand beyond what we have known or already created.

Fire has its place. Its place is not in the beginning stages of evolution, when stability and steadfastness are being learned. The qualities of fire—courage, extroversion, independence, initiative, and physical strength—can be dangerous unless we have gained some basic stability and emotional development. Because of this, fire is usually not chosen in the early cycles except to teach a particular lesson or balance dependency. Not until the Mature cycle are we apt to choose several lifetimes with the fire signs to expand our potentials.

When we first experience fire, we usually express it crudely and awkwardly. This is true of all the elements. However, fire has the potential of being more destructive than the other elements. It is expressive and active, and when expression and action are ill advised or poorly executed, the results can be devastating. Because of this, we may incur more karma in our first lifetimes with fire than with any other element.

Although it is unusual, when a fire sign is needed in the Baby and Young cycle, Aries is the one chosen because of its physical strength and prowess. These qualities, along with its strong ego, aid survival. Furthermore, Aries, like Capricorn, develops the self-reliance and self-sufficiency needed in the early cycles. Aries is less helpful in the late Baby and Young cycles, though, because a major task then is bonding with family and community. However, it may be useful then in transforming the dependency of many Cancer or Piscean lifetimes into caring for others. Leo and Sagittarius are not particularly helpful in the Baby and Young cycles because they do not enhance survival or relationships.

Aries serves several purposes in the Mature cycle, even when the life task does not entail leadership and exploration. It energizes our goals and drives us to expand our potentials. It also fuels the drive to explore inner frontiers, so important in this cycle. Aries, or less often the other fire signs, may also be used to overcome dependency or fearfulness. This explains why some Arians do not appear Arian. Of course, Aries is also chosen by Mature souls whose life task entails scientific investigation, exploration, athletic prowess, business ventures, promotion, sales, political leadership, or inventing new products or technology.

Leading and teaching are common to both Leo and the Mature cycle, making Leo a favorite choice for this cycle. The self-exploration and self-development of this cycle also make Leo just the sign for this cycle. Many develop their creative talents during this cycle by choosing Leo. However, Leo does not reflect the inward, psychological, and spiritual bent of the Mature cycle. As for Sagittarius, Mature and Old souls choose it more frequently than any other sign except Pisces and Scorpio because it meets both their need for self-development and for understanding.

During the Old cycle, the fire signs are favorites for the same reasons they are in the Mature cycle. In this cycle, fire signs continue to be used to motivate us to develop our talents and other potentials. Moreover, fire signs encourage leadership, which is needed by many of this cycle's life tasks. Without them, Old souls might avoid leadership and authority.

Air

Air signs play a role in each of the cycles, but they are not as common in the Baby and Young cycles as in the Mature and Old cycles. Air is needed to develop the intellect, sociability, and powers of reason. Even though the intellect plays an important role in our survival, it is less important in the Baby cycle than other things. Air is most important in the Young cycle for its ability to strengthen family and community relationships. It is also useful for intellectual development in this cycle. As the intellect develops, so do our opinions and ideas, which separate and distinguish us from others. During the Baby and Young cycles, we hold our ideas as if they were law, with some difficulty seeing other points of view. The polarization of ideas during this cycle stimulates our thought processes, and exercises our discrimination and logical analysis.

Gemini is a favorite sign in the Young cycle. The Young cycle is a time for exploring ideas, people, and different ways of being in the world. It is analogous to young adulthood, when we are discovering who we are. Gemini suits this cycle more than any other sign because it provides the curiosity and motivation to examine many facets of life. In this cycle, Gemini is chosen to sample life before settling down to one specific talent or set of life tasks. After the Young cycle, we are ready to choose a more specific direction.

Libra is another favorite sign of the Young cycle for its ability to strengthen love and bonding with a partner. The beginnings of personal love begin in the late Baby and the Young cycle, following earlier dependency.

Aquarius is chosen infrequently in the Young cycle and even less frequently in the Baby cycle. Its progressiveness and unconventionality are not advantageous in either cycle, when conservatism and caution are needed to develop the means for survival and the family relationships important to emotional growth. When Aquarius is chosen in the Young cycle, it is usually for furthering our social conscience and group participation, which may be necessary if we are failing to develop naturally in these ways.

Gemini may be chosen in the Mature cycle if the life task requires intellectual refinement, improved communication skills, or extensive study of a particular subject, which many do. Gemini may also be chosen if the life task involves communication, teaching, learning, or transportation. The flightiness and superficiality of Gemini is likely to be less apparent in this cycle than in the earlier ones, and the verbal and communicative side of Gemini more apparent.

When Libra is chosen in the Mature cycle, it is usually to develop artistic abilities or aesthetic appreciation, or to increase our ability to love. Because Libra teaches the lessons of personal love and relationship, it is chosen as often as needed during the various cycles. Libra is most emphasized in the Young and Mature cycles, but if necessary, the lessons continue into the Old. Sometime in the Old cycle, we develop the capacity for unconditional love. At that point, the lessons in personal love diminish and greater focus is placed on the life task. However, those who have delayed the lessons of love because they have been developing a certain talent or quality will need to concentrate on these lessons in the Old cycle.

Aquarius is likely to be chosen in the Mature cycle by those whose life tasks pertain to new discoveries, new ideas, advances in technology, humanitarian reform, politics, or a team or group endeavors. Since the Mature cycle is a time of strengthening our intuition and creativity, Aquarius may also be chosen for this. Not until the Old cycle, however, does the intuition begin to be consistently available to us.

Air signs are favored in the Old cycle, as they are in the Mature cycle, for providing the intellectual development for highly complex tasks. Aquarius is the air sign most favored in the Old cycle because it supplies intuition, the desire to serve humanity, and the vision for what is needed for the betterment of humanity.

CHAPTER 4

THE ROLE AND ORIGIN OF ASPECTS IN THE CHART

Aspects play a minor role in chart analysis in the sense that the themes, the lessons, and the life task can all be determined without even examining them. However, they are important in more specific chart analysis. Besides substantiating the information about the lessons and life task, they often describe major psychological issues and the circumstances responsible for them in former lifetimes.

Some aspects are chosen and some are acquired. Sometimes an aspect is chosen, like the signs, to supply an energy for the lessons or the life task. Others are present because they reflect negative behaviors or attitudes learned in former lifetimes that need balancing. These behaviors or attitudes often stem from a traumatic incident, though some are simply bad habits.

The first question to ask in aspect analysis, then, concerns the aspect's origin. Was it chosen to help with the lessons or the life task, or does it reflect a pattern from former lifetimes that needs to be changed? The answer to this question will determine how challenging the aspect will be. Aspects we have chosen will be less challenging and less apparent than those symbolizing entrenched patterns, which represent our most formidable psychological issues. Because of this, and because of the general lack of information about the relationship between aspects and past-life patterns, special care will be taken in this chapter to address aspects that reflect entrenched patterns. In summary, aspects play four roles:

1. They are chosen to support the themes. They work in conjunction with the signs and other chart factors to describe the strengths and bring about the lessons.

2. They are chosen to supply a quality, an attitude, or an approach needed in the life task.

3. They are chosen as an added challenge to accelerate one's evolution.

4. They represent a behavior or attitude established in a former lifetime or lifetimes stemming from trauma or habit.

Every aspect is either chosen or acquired to serve one or more of these functions. Only intuition can determine what that function is. An aspect's strength varies from chart to chart as well, and also can be determined only intuitively.

When an aspect is playing the first role, it is merely reiterating a theme stated in the signs and serving the same function as the signs in supplying the energy needed for the lessons and the life task. When it is serving this purpose, it fits with the themes. For example, numerous aspects to Uranus may support an Aquarian theme.

Aspects serving this role also provide information about the degree of development of the signs and how they are being expressed. Planets ruling less-developed signs are likely to be involved in a greater number of challenging aspects: squares, inconjuncts, oppositions, and difficult conjunctions. Planets ruling signs representing strengths are likely to be involved in more trines, sextiles, and harmonious conjunctions.

For instance, someone with Aquarius (ruled by Uranus) and Cancer (ruled by the Moon) themes is not likely to express both signs equally well since they are so different. If he or she has several Uranus squares, a Uranus/Mars conjunction, a Cancer Moon in the fourth house, a Neptune/Moon trine, and a Jupiter/Moon conjunction, Cancer is probably more developed than Aquarius. However, the difference may be mild or marked. Of course, a sign is often represented both positively and negatively in the aspects. When this is the case, the sign is probably being refined, and it will be expressed inconsistently.

Squares, inconjuncts, oppositions, and difficult conjunctions between the personal planets and the outer planets (Saturn, Uranus, Neptune, and Pluto) are most likely to indicate our lessons and most difficult challenges. If an aspect involves *only* outer planets (Saturn, Uranus, Neptune, or Pluto), it is not as likely to indicate a lesson as when a personal planet (the Sun, the Moon, Mercury, Venus, or Mars) or the Ascendant is also involved. Difficult conjunctions can be as challenging as squares and oppositions. A list of difficult and easy conjunctions is included under "Conjunctions."

The second role—supplying a quality, an attitude, or an approach needed in the life task—is similar to the first role in providing something the individual needs. Every life task must be backed up by chart factors that provide the skills, energy, and motivation to accomplish it. Aspects that play this role usually reflect talents and strengths already developed in former lifetimes. If, for example, the life task involves healing, aspects such as the Moon trine Neptune, Sun conjunct Mercury, and Jupiter trine Mercury may be chosen to provide the skills and inclination to pursue a career in healing. Neptune trine the Moon gives the compassion and desire to serve. The Sun conjunct Mercury, and Jupiter trine Mercury, give the necessary mental and technical skills. These are not challenging aspects, but challenging aspects may also be useful to the life task and chosen for that purpose.

Challenging aspects create inner stress, which can motivate us to take action or attain skills useful in the life task. Challenging Pluto aspects provide the desire for control and self-mastery needed to transform others and ourselves. They are ideal for life tasks involving healing. Challenging Saturn aspects supply the drive and determination needed for great accomplishments. With these aspects, we feel a deep sense of personal responsibility and guilt or fear, and the need to achieve something meaningful to set things right. Challenging Neptune aspects provide a struggle with being in the world that helps us come to grips with the meaning of life and our role in the greater scheme. They develop our compassion and spiritual understanding. Challenging Uranus aspects cause us to look at things in an unusual or unconventional manner, which encourages new discoveries or new approaches.

An aspect may also be chosen to provide an extra challenge, which forces us to work harder and push ourselves beyond our ordinary limits, thereby strengthening us in ways we might not otherwise have been strengthened. A challenging aspect does this by providing a character flaw, a problem, or a difficult event that must be overcome. The strengths that are gained from overcoming this difficulty become gifts to be used in the life task or to help others overcome similar difficulties. Those who choose more than their share of challenges are taking a harder path, but one potentially full of rewards and satisfaction.

The fourth role aspects play is in describing a behavior, an attitude, or an approach established in former lifetimes that needs to be changed. There are two reasons these patterns form. The first is that the behavior or attitude may have been useful temporarily in helping to cope with a trauma, so it is clung to unconsciously. The second reason for these patterns is habit. A habit may have been formed by choosing a sign repeatedly and not choosing a counterpart to balance it, or by not integrating the countering energy sufficiently. A habit formed over many lifetimes can be especially hard to change because motivation may be lacking, since it may not be seen as a problem.

THE ASPECTS

Before defining the aspects, it is important to note that the difference between the challenging or hard aspects (squares, inconjuncts, oppositions, and difficult conjunctions) and the harmonious or soft ones (trines, sextiles, and harmonious conjunctions) may be minimal. In the chart of someone who is advanced, there may be little difference between a square and a trine, for example. This is because, as we evolve, we learn to express even our challenging aspects positively. Therefore, the less advanced we are, the more likely our challenging aspects are to operate negatively.

Also, whether a challenging aspect is experienced as an event or as an inner conflict depends on our relationship to change, how perceptive and intuitive we are, and how willing we are to experience change from within rather than externally. People grow differently: some create changes in their outer circumstances in response to their inner conflicts, while others change internally as a result of outer changes. Of course, we all grow by both means, but one style usually predominates.

Conjunctions

The conjunction is the most powerful of all the aspects. It produces a blending or interaction of the energies involved. The energies involved in a conjunction must be considered together, as they do not function separately from each other. Conjunctions that involve the Sun, the Moon, Ascendant, Mercury, Venus, or Mars are always significant and mark dynamic expressions of energy, which stand out in the individual's personality.

The conjunction can function positively or negatively depending on the planets involved. If the planets are compatible and similar in nature, their conjunction can strengthen the planets' positive qualities, resulting in greater gifts than if those planets functioned separately. On the other hand, if the planets are antagonistic or opposite in nature, their conjunction is likely to represent a significant challenge. In that case, the planets' positive energies may be harder to release and the negative energies more readily expressed, especially if the planets negatively reinforce each other (e.g., Mars and Pluto). However, someone who is advanced may express even a difficult conjunction well. How the conjunction is aspected in the chart is another factor that influences how it will function. Even a Jupiter/Sun conjunction may be expressed negatively if it has challenging aspects to it.

Difficult Planetary Conjunctions

Sun: Sun/Saturn

Moon: Moon/Mars, Moon/Saturn, Moon/Uranus

Mercury: Mercury/Neptune

Venus: Venus/Saturn, Venus/Uranus

Mars: Mars/Moon, Mars/Saturn, Mars/Uranus, Mars/Neptune

Saturn: Saturn/Sun, Saturn/Moon, Saturn/Venus, Saturn/Mars, Saturn/Neptune, Saturn/Pluto

Uranus: Uranus/Moon, Uranus/Venus, Uranus/Mars

Neptune: Neptune/Mercury, Neptune/Mars, Neptune/Saturn

Pluto: Pluto/Saturn

Easy Planetary Conjunctions

Sun: Sun/Mercury, Sun/Venus, Sun/Jupiter

Moon: Moon/Venus, Moon/Jupiter

Mercury: Mercury/Sun, Mercury/Venus, Mercury/Jupiter, Mercury/Uranus

Venus: Venus/Sun, Venus/Moon, Venus/Mercury, Venus/Jupiter

Mars: Mars/Jupiter

Jupiter: Jupiter/Sun, Jupiter/Moon, Jupiter/Venus, Jupiter/Mars

Uranus: Uranus/Mercury

Conjunctions that are not listed could be difficult or not, depending on other factors.

Sextiles

Sextiles represent positive potentials or opportunities that can be tapped with some effort and energy. Sextiles are present in the chart to strengthen certain tendencies and encourage development in a certain direction. They are related to the life task in that they are chosen to ease and encourage movement toward the life task, but their gifts may or may not be applied directly to it. They could be thought of as gifts or talents in-the-making. The gifts represented by the sextile are the gifts of the signs and planets involved in the sextile.

Trines

Trines represent our resources. These resources seem like gifts, but they have been earned through efforts in former lifetimes. Usually, these gifts were developed from previous life tasks and are therefore likely to be used in the current life task. The gifts represented by the trines may be taken for granted and go unrecognized, however, especially when numerous trines and few challenging aspects are present. We often don't recognize our strengths unless others point them out to us. It is easy to assume that everyone has the same ease with something that we do, and unless we are challenged to use our strengths by circumstances, they may lie dormant.

The gifts represented by the trine are the gifts of the signs and planets involved in the trine. The planets in a trine do not conflict with each other but work together to produce a positive synergy. Unless the planets involved are otherwise afflicted, they are likely to bring out the best in each other.

Oppositions

Oppositions represent potential growth or awareness resulting from contact or conflict with others. The opposition manifests mostly through relationships and produces growth through expanded awareness of various viewpoints. The conflict with others that this aspect brings mirrors an internal conflict, which calls for awareness and resolution. The resolution of an opposition usually requires a compromise. This aspect pulls the individual in two opposite directions represented by the signs and houses it is placed in, and a middle ground must be found. Both sides of the opposition need to be honored, owned, and expressed positively. The pull created by the opposition is not always that stressful, however. Sometimes the opposition represents two different approaches that are easily combined and integrated, resulting in a synthesis of two different viewpoints or approaches. This synthesis is the gift of the opposition.

How stressful an opposition is depends on the planets involved and the individual's development. If the planetary energies are very different, they may be difficult to integrate into a coherent approach. If that is the case, the individual will either block the expression of one of the planets, project one of the planets onto someone else, or alternate between expressing one and then the other planet in the opposition. The negative side of each planet in an opposition tends to be expressed until they are integrated or a compromise position is found.

Squares

Squares can be the most difficult of all the aspects because they usually link energies from very different signs. The planets involved in a square interfere with or block each other's expression, which creates tension and usually brings out the worst in each of the planets involved until the tension is resolved. The planetary drives work at cross-purposes, which makes it difficult to get both needs, as represented by the signs and houses, met. Still, the goal is to find a way to meet both needs without denying either planet's needs. The effort required to do this, though not always easy or pleasant, is productive and results in special gifts. The internal conflict and external stress created by the square motivate us to make strides in our growth that we might not otherwise have made. Consequently, squares are common in the charts of many of the most successful people.

More than any other aspect, squares are likely to represent troublesome psychological issues and patterns from the past, especially if Saturn or Pluto is involved. If a square represents such an issue or pattern, it may describe the main challenge of the chart. On the other hand, some squares represent issues or patterns that are nearly transformed through efforts in other lifetimes, leaving little left to be balanced. Some are simply chosen to supply a certain energy. When either of the latter is the case, the square may have little impact.

The stressfulness of a square also depends on the planets and signs involved. Squares involving planets similar in nature are less stressful than those involving dissimilar energies. Squares involving the same elements, as happens from time to time, are only mildly stressful, but still connect the energies of the two planets. Most importantly, the stressfulness of a square depends on the individual's development and maturity.

The T-Square is a special kind of square made up of an opposition and a planet at right angles to that opposition. This configuration is likely to represent a person's most challenging psychological issues and also his or her greatest talents, which arise from dealing with the challenge. The planet squaring the opposition is highly important and may represent both the main challenge and the greatest gift of the chart.

Inconjuncts (Quincunxes)

The inconjunct represents a minor irritation in one's psychological makeup. However, it feels anything but minor if it is repeated in other chart factors. The inconjunct is not of primary importance in delineating the chart because anything it says of psychological relevance will be stated in other chart factors.

The inconjunct does play an important role in karmic analysis of the chart, however. The planets and the signs (and sometimes the houses) involved in the inconjunct describe an incident from a former lifetime whose influence will be met in the current one. The incident may or may not relate to the chart's major lessons, but its effects will be evident to some degree in the individual's psychology. Some examples of this will be given later.

INTERPRETING THE ASPECTS

Interpreting an aspect is a process of synthesizing: 1) the kind of aspect; 2) the signs involved; 3) the planets involved; 4) the houses involved; 5) the aspect's origin and purpose; and 6) the individual's development.

Aspects connect houses, signs, and planets to describe a personality trait or a gift. If the personality trait described does not reflect an ingrained pattern from the past, but was chosen to direct growth or aid the life task, it will not have much negative impact on the personality. Aspects that perform this function may be either hard or soft depending on what energies are needed and what areas of life need to be included. When a square is serving the function of connecting certain houses, it will not be especially stressful. Trines and other harmonious aspects are also used to connect certain planets, signs, and houses, but they do so in a more predictably nonproblematic way.

Let's look at an example of how an aspect might help with the life task. Suppose someone has a highly intellectual life task, which requires Gemini in his chart, and which was prepared for in many previous lifetimes by also having Gemini in the chart. Unfortunately, in his previous lifetimes, he developed the habit of not completing his projects. To help him overcome this, Pluto square Sun has been chosen in this lifetime to supply perseverance and focus. Although the usual interpretation of Pluto square Sun is willfulness, it may also be chosen to add will to a personality that lacks it. Thus, aspects sometimes represent qualities we do not have but need.

Knowing why an aspect is in the chart—in this case, whether it reflects willfulness or was chosen to balance a lack of focus—is critical in understanding how it will operate and how stressful it will be. In this example, a Pluto/Sun square is not problematic. This illustrates how important it is to consider the entire chart when interpreting an aspect. Each aspect must be assessed according to how alike or different it is from the rest of the chart. Of course, the Pluto/Sun square in this chart could just as well indicate willfulness, and the Gemini could have been chosen to balance that. We can usually discover which interpretation is correct by finding out more about the person.

The house placement of the Pluto/Sun aspect shows us where he is likely to meet the energy of this square. With his Sun in Capricorn in the tenth house and Pluto in Libra in the seventh house, he is likely to experience a business partnership or a marriage with someone who is forceful, persevering, and strong— someone who can model the qualities he needs or help him develop them through conflict.

Let's take another example, this time, to illustrate how aspects may be chosen to help with the life lesson. Suppose someone has Piscean gifts but lacks discrimination and mental focus, common faults of Pisceans. If the life task depends on Piscean talents, Pisces cannot be eliminated from the chart, but other signs and chart factors could balance its negative tendencies.

For example, Saturn opposite Mercury in Pisces would slow the mind and discipline it, giving it a more practical and realistic approach, while still allowing it to function intuitively. Because Saturn would also be in Virgo, this would further balance the intuition with logic and analysis. By tying Saturn to Mercury and Virgo to Pisces by opposition, the individual could experience the benefits of a more balanced and discriminating mind. What the individual learned from this would carry over into later lifetimes.

We have seen that not all squares, inconjuncts, oppositions, and difficult conjunctions reflect a major psychological issue or challenge. When they do, they may represent our core challenge or what may stand in the way of our life task. Most of our difficult psychological issues originate in past lives. The next section looks more closely at these important psychological aspects, showing how they originate and how they can be distinguished from aspects such as those just described that direct growth or aid the life task.

ASPECTS THAT ORIGINATE IN PAST LIVES

These aspects reflect past-life patterns and psychological issues that may interfere with fulfilling our potential. However, even they may be fairly mild and nonproblematic. Some hold only minimal power because they have been worked through in recent lifetimes, and others were never strong to begin with. The stories that follow, of people living today, illustrate how these kinds of aspects operate.

In a former lifetime, Janet experienced a traumatic death at the hands of her enraged lover. Many seriously inhibiting psychological issues are rooted in past-life tragedies or traumatic deaths like this one. Before each incarnation, we select something to heal, and a chart and circumstances to heal it, until all the traumas from our past are mended. Janet's soul chose to work through this particular trauma, represented in her chart by Pluto (death) square Venus (love).

This incident undermined Janet's confidence, sense of worth, and trust in fellow human beings. These feelings currently manifest as suspicion, jealousy, and the need to possess and control those she loves. This pattern is still deeply entrenched and will probably take several lifetimes to heal. To aid her healing, her soul chose a Libra Moon and a Scorpio Sun. With the luminaries in these signs, avoiding relationships will not be an option. In having to face her insecurities, Janet is likely to conquer them. Let's look at another example.

Bob is unable to perform effectively in positions of responsibility and authority because of an experience in a past life in which his caretakers belittled him for being retarded. The aspect that reflects this challenge is a T-Square with Saturn in the third house, Mercury in the seventh house, and the Moon in the ninth house. The Moon opposite Saturn in these houses symbolizes Bob's deep-seated insecurity about intellectual matters. Mercury in the seventh house square this opposition describes his difficulty forming relationships as a result. This configuration not only describes

Bob's challenge, but also the circumstances responsible for it: the Moon relates to his caretakers; Saturn, to the betrayal he felt; and Mercury, to his mental disability.

Bob's challenge is to overcome his sense of shame and inferiority. To help him with this, his soul chose a fiery chart for confidence and a Grand Trine in earth, making material success and the respect that comes with it more likely.

Chris is in his late thirties and has never had a meaningful love relationship. Seeing his mother and father torment each other in a former lifetime left a psychic impression, which has affected Chris's current relationships, despite his current parents' positive relationship. The aspect representing this is Venus square Uranus. For him, this does not represent fear of intimacy as much as his belief that intimate relationships are untrustworthy and, therefore, not worthwhile. Chris will need people, events, and circumstances to help him learn the deep rewards of intimacy and relationship. With a Cancer Moon trine a Scorpio Sun, life is bound to provide him with the wholesome and rewarding nurturing experiences he needs to overcome this attitude.

In examining aspects that originate in the past, the inconjunct is worthy of special attention. More consistently than any other aspect, the inconjunct describes an experience from a past life that must be balanced. The inconjunct is one way the soul attempts to balance, or erase from the psyche, unfortunate past-life experiences. The planets and signs involved describe a past-life incident or experience that corresponds to a psychological complex. The houses involved usually describe the area of life in which the psychological complex will be most apparent and how it will most likely be balanced. Sometimes the houses, like the planets and signs, also describe the circumstances responsible for the complex, but only when those circumstances are the same as what is needed for it to be balanced. The two stories that follow show how an inconjunct might originate.

In a past life, Jim encountered a particularly frightening event, which he responded to by withdrawing into mental illness. This is represented in his current chart by an inconjunct between Mars and Neptune, reflecting his inner conflict over aggression. To help him discontinue this pattern of dealing with difficulties, his soul chose an Aries Sun and Ascendant in the hope that he would gain some courage and regain an appreciation for assertiveness.

When faced with overwhelming physical pain in a former lifetime, John surrendered his ego, not to mental illness, but to Cosmic Consciousness. Unfortunately, this actually inhibited his growth because he used it to glorify himself in that lifetime. Mars inconjunct Neptune in John's chart represents his former improper use of power (Mars) in relation to spiritual matters (Neptune).

Jim's and John's stories illustrate the complexity of aspect analysis. Besides the fact that aspects serve four different functions in a chart, aspects that originate in the past stem from an infinite variety of events and, therefore, have many possible interpretations. Aspect interpretation is the most challenging part of chart interpretation. It requires excellent intuition, especially when past-life incidents and issues are involved.

ASPECTS WITH THE OUTER PLANETS

Challenging aspects between the personal planets (the Sun, the Moon, Mercury, Venus, and Mars) and the outer ones (Saturn, Uranus, Neptune, and Pluto) describe our major psychological issues more often than any other kind of aspect. Because aspects between the personal and outer planets are often so important, the next section describes these aspects according to the kind of aspect (hard or soft) and its role.

The four roles mentioned earlier have been combined under two for simplification: aspects that represent patterns from the past and aspects that supply a needed energy. The other roles— providing an additional challenge (which functions like a past-life pattern) and supplying energy for the life task—fall under these two categories but were initially presented separately for greater clarification. Please remember that this information is only a guideline; it won't hold true for every chart.

Hard Aspects to Saturn That Represent Patterns from the Past

These aspects are characterized by fear. The fear usually pertains to issues related to the planet Saturn is aspecting. The fear is often irrational, unexplainable by current circumstances, and deep-seated. Many people with these aspects are not even aware of the extent of their fear because they have never known life without it. This is one reason it can be hard to overcome. Those who are aware of it are ashamed of it, and this eats away at their self-esteem.

Challenging Saturn aspects, especially those with the Sun or the Moon, are some of the most difficult to overcome. When our self-esteem is undermined, as it is with these aspects, it can be difficult to summon the motivation to conquer what we fear. These Saturn aspects, like all Saturn aspects, make us stronger if we do not fall prey to pessimism, negativity, and feelings of inferiority. Facing our fears strengthens us, and the courage that we gain can help us face other fears. Saturn is the Great Teacher. Much of what it teaches cannot be learned any other way than through hard work, responsibility, persistence, and patience, the qualities developed by these aspects.

Challenging Saturn aspects are justifiably characterized by fear. They usually have their origin in traumatic past-life events in which we were powerless to protect ourselves from death or a tragic loss. In these circumstances, we may have been killed or watched helplessly while someone else was killed. Traumatic deaths leave strong imprints on our psyche. They impress us with our vulnerability. This sense of vulnerability and powerlessness is what remains in the psyche of someone who has experienced a traumatic death. It is reflected in the chart as a challenging Saturn aspect, related by planet, house, or sign to the trauma's cause.

We all experience many traumatic deaths over the course of our many lifetimes. The soul has the task of arranging future lifetimes that will help us work through these traumatic experiences. It does so carefully and systematically by selecting one trauma at a time. This trauma may be reflected in a hard Saturn aspect.

A challenging Saturn aspect may also portray a fearful or unfortunate event in the current lifetime. It may symbolize the loss of someone we love (when Venus is involved), inadequate or harsh parenting (when the Sun or the Moon is involved), abuse or violence (when Mars is involved), or a learning or speech problem (when Mercury is involved), to name only a few possibilities. Thus, challenging Saturn aspects may represent past traumatic deaths or near death experiences, or similar experiences, or other unfortunate events in the current lifetime. If the individual has irrational fears, the aspect undoubtedly relates to a past-life experience. If the experience is yet to come, it serves no purpose to discuss it.

An astrologer should never predict a tragic event. Events like these that can be seen in the chart are inevitable and serve a purpose in the life Plan. Describing the possibilities would only create fear. Besides, you may be wrong. We must keep in mind that the purpose of these universal experiences is to strengthen us. Saturn is not here to teach us that Death is victor and we are nothing. It is here to teach us that life is precious and that we are more than our lives. The strength acquired from facing our fears and moving beyond them is an added bonus.

When a challenging Saturn aspect represents a past trauma, the story of the traumatic incident can be seen in the planets, signs, and houses involved in the Saturn aspect by synthesizing these factors. Undeniably, excellent intuition is needed for this. Here's a story that illustrates how a traumatic incident might be described by an aspect.

In a former lifetime, Jeremy had the unfortunate experience of being eaten by a tiger: while hunting, he was hunted. This experience is reflected in irrational nighttime fears. Although the hunt did not happen in the dark, in a little boy's imagination (Jeremy is currently a little boy) the dark is a fertile backdrop for his projected fears. Interestingly, Jeremy has found some comfort in having his pet cat sleep with him at night. This may sound contradictory in light of his past. However, the soul often gently introduces whatever caused our fear into our current experience to help us overcome it.

This unfortunate event is noted in Jeremy's chart as Saturn in Sagittarius in the fifth house square Mars in Pisces in the eighth house. Saturn in Sagittarius in the fifth house represents the adventurer who got burned, who now lacks courage and confidence. Mars in Pisces in the eighth house refers to the death, with the eighth house symbolizing death, and Mars in Pisces symbolizing the rechanneling of his aggressive energies into spiritual understanding. The result of any death is a greater understanding of our vulnerability and the realization that we are much more than our vulnerable bodies. At the time of his death, he felt unconquerable; he trusted his body and senses too much. For him, this event provided an important spiritual lesson, represented by Mars in Pisces.

In this lifetime, Mars in Pisces is likely to be experienced as sensitivity to other realms—to the spiritual side of life. This is the gift of this aspect. The square to Saturn implies some internal struggle before this sensitivity is appreciated. In Jeremy's case, the internal struggle is likely to entail questions about his masculinity, and what it means to be courageous and strong. Ultimately, he is likely to conclude that true strength does not lie in physical strength alone but in spiritual strength.

Hard Aspects to Saturn That Supply a Needed Energy

This is the other role that challenging Saturn aspects play in a chart. These aspects supply saturnine qualities to the area of life symbolized by the personal planet involved in the aspect. For example, Saturn square Venus supplies the saturnine qualities of loyalty and steadfastness to relationships. Fear and an overly serious attitude toward relationships may also result from this aspect, but only if it serves a purpose, perhaps by delaying involvement in love affairs to allow the person to work on the life task or balance a karmic debt. When challenging aspects serve this role, they will not be as stressful as when they originate from a past-life trauma. Here's a story that illustrates this.

Albert's life task involves creating a business that will benefit his community. In his chart, the North Node in the second house in Aquarius represents this. He also has several planets in Taurus in the fifth house, Capricorn rising, and a Libra Moon. In former lifetimes, his business ventures were impractical, as symbolized by a conjunction of the Moon and Neptune. The South Node in Leo exemplifies a past-life pattern of pursuing self-expression and creativity.

In this lifetime, Albert is challenged to find a way to apply his creativity practically. This practicality is achieved through the aspects and earth signs. The trine between his Capricorn Ascendant and most of the planets in Taurus strengthens the positive earthy qualities of these signs. Saturn conjunct his Moon and Neptune, and square his Ascendant adds further earthiness. In part, he acquired this practicality by having to grow up fast (Saturn conjunct Moon and Neptune) as a result of inadequate mothering.

Soft Aspects to Saturn

"Soft" or "harmonious" aspects are the trine, the sextile, and some conjunctions. Trines represent talents or positive qualities developed over many lifetimes, which appear as gifts. However, these gifts vary in development. Every trine does not represent a highly developed talent or quality, although it does represent a certain level of attainment in relationship to the lessons of the planet involved. Soft conjunctions may also represent talents and positive qualities, and may function more forcefully than trines. On the other hand, they may simply supply a needed energy. Sextiles represent talents in the making—no more, no less. They are the simplest, most straightforward aspects to interpret.

The talents that are symbolized by Saturn trines, sextiles, and some conjunctions are abilities and attitudes that were formed from overcoming the trials, delays, frustrations, and difficulties of dealing with the material realm. No one escapes these trials. Regardless of our level of development, we all must face the limitations of the material world. Virtues such as patience, perseverance, caution, thoroughness, pride in accomplishment, and endurance develop from successfully dealing with the material realm.

Although some of Saturn's virtues are developed without hardship and struggle, Saturn's gifts are not. The ability to foresee problems and avoid them through planning, to work long and hard regardless of reward, and to support ourselves in an uncertain universe are just some of these gifts. Through Saturn's hardships we develop the perseverance to develop our character and talents. Saturn provides the primary lessons of life upon which other development rests.

Soft aspects to Saturn combine these positive saturnine qualities with whatever sign, house, or planet it is aspecting. For example, Saturn trine the Moon in Gemini in the seventh house gives loyalty in one's relationships. Saturn conjunct Venus in Aries in the second house gives discipline and determination in regard to one's artistic talents. Saturn trine the Sun in Pisces in the third house gives focus, discipline, and practicality to an idealistic and intuitive mind.

Harmonious Saturn aspects describe the areas of life to which we most readily apply positive Saturnine qualities and ones likely to be important to our life task. Challenging Saturn aspects supply saturnine energy, indicate the need to develop saturnine qualities, or represent a lesson or fear. How, then, do we interpret the complexity created by all of Saturn's aspects? Let's look at some examples to see how to synthesize the factors related to Saturn.

Saturn heavily influences Peter's chart. Saturn is conjunct the Midheaven in Taurus, opposite Venus and Mars in Scorpio in the fourth house, and square the Moon and Pluto in Virgo in the first house. One theme we find is Venus combined with Saturn: Venus is opposite Saturn, and Saturn is in Taurus, whose ruler is Venus. Another theme combines the Moon and Scorpio: the Moon is conjunct Pluto, the ruler of Scorpio; and Scorpio rules the fourth house, naturally ruled by the Moon. If we put this information together, we come up with something like this: Peter will be challenged to grow because of his need for emotional closeness, sexuality, and family, particularly in ways that affect his work habits.

With Saturn in Taurus conjunct the Midheaven, Peter needs a secure position in the world, one that provides the structure and routine that will develop the qualities of Taurus: hard work, dependability, and endurance. With Venus and Mars in Scorpio in the fourth house squaring his Moon/Pluto conjunction in the first house, he will seek a partner who will demand emotional closeness and help him cultivate this within himself. His challenge is to meet his need for family and emotional closeness, develop his work-related skills, and find fulfillment in doing that. The T-Square shows these aspects of life—work, family, and self-development—vying for his energy.

Peter married young and began his family immediately. As a young man, his need for closeness, as represented by the planets in Scorpio, superseded self-development. This may be a source of conflict for him later, when this T-Square is transited. With the Moon in the first house (identity) as the focus of the T-Square, it is not surprising that his identity is being sacrificed to meet the needs of the other portions of the T-Square. This is common with the focal planet in a T-Square. It is especially not surprising, since the Moon in Virgo in the first house represents a blending of his personal needs with the needs of others, the family in particular, and a need to serve his family. Pluto conjunct the Moon repeats the Scorpio/Moon theme, representing the draw of emotions, sexuality, and family in his life. This conjunction also indicates that the area of life ruled by the Moon will be a source of transformation for him, shaping and molding him, and teaching him about love and commitment. So, Saturn in Taurus on the Midheaven is likely to represent the sacrifices he will make in his career to properly care for his wife and children.

Claire is unable to speak or write clearly because of a recent stroke. Before that, she was a writer who enjoyed a long, successful career. Saturn is part of a third-house stellium (three or more planets that are conjunct) in Gemini, including the Moon, Mercury, and Pluto. This stellium represents both her gifts and her challenge. Saturn and Pluto add seriousness and pessimism to the usually lighthearted and superficial Gemini planets, bringing focus, determination, and perseverance to her mind and emotions.

This stellium was very challenging to Claire in her youth. When other youngsters were playing with dolls and riding bicycles, she was contemplating the meaning of life—and death. Claire's mother died when she was small (Saturn and Pluto conjunct the Moon), leaving her with a sense of failure, loss, and unworthiness (Saturn conjunct Moon).

To right this, Claire set out to understand her mother's death by studying religion, metaphysics, psychic phenomena, and reincarnation. In her adult years, she was instrumental in bringing a new understanding about death to many who were dying, and to their loved ones. Although her stroke may seem ironic and unfair, it provides her with an opportunity to experience life from another level, one less attached to ego, language, and conditioned ways of thinking. Claire's exploration of the mysteries of life has not been curtailed; it is just taking a different form.

Keith is a middle-aged man who owns a business that manufactures clothing. Keith's business is thriving now only after many years of struggle. He not only built a successful company from scratch, but he also provided employment to many who might otherwise have been unemployed. This was critical in releasing a karmic debt he owed to several people.

The debt is depicted in Keith's chart by a T-Square in the mutable signs, with Saturn in Virgo in the second house opposite Mars in Pisces in the eighth house, and the Moon in Sagittarius in the fifth house. Saturn opposite Mars represents his failure to protect his employees, which resulted in their injury.

His chart also gives him the resources to balance this debt. The Moon in Sagittarius in the fifth house gives him the confidence and courage to start a business. Mars in Pisces in the eighth house gives him financial insight. Saturn in Virgo gives him a practical and thorough approach, and Venus and Mercury in Aquarius foster concern for the welfare of others.

It should be obvious from these examples that chart interpretation, particularly of the aspects, is largely intuitive. Yet, in most cases, the aspects do not have to be delineated to this degree. These examples were not offered to illustrate that readings should include this kind of specificity, but to show how the aspects in a chart work.

Uranus Aspects

The subject matter and examples in this section are bound to be lighter because of the nature of Uranus and the different role it plays than Saturn. Uranus encourages us to go beyond our ordinary behavior and try new things. It brings excitement, openness to change, and daring to whatever planet or area of life it is influencing. Whether a Uranus aspect is hard or soft is less significant than with Saturn, Pluto, or even Neptune aspects. Uranus brings the same openness to the new regardless of the aspect. How a Uranus aspect will be expressed has more to do with development and the remainder of the chart than with the aspect.

Uranus aspects play an important and unique role in our evolution. Their role is unique because the openness to change associated with them is not felt constantly but only when stimulated by transits. The more Uranus aspects there are, the less this is true, however. Those with many Uranus aspects may have them to induce constant change and variety in their lives, usually to help with the life task or lessons. Most people have no more than two major Uranus aspects (involving personal planets or the Ascendant), which lie dormant, as far as stimulating change, until transited.

Uranus transits often bring changes in one area of life that have repercussions in other areas. Sometimes, in fact, the initial changes brought about by Uranus are insignificant to our growth compared to their repercussions. Often, the real point of a Uranus transit is overlooked or misunderstood by astrologers because the event that catalyzed the change is assumed to be central. The next story illustrates this.

Mark was born with Uranus conjunct his Midheaven in Taurus and making no other aspects in his chart. During his midlife crisis, when transiting Uranus opposed his natal Uranus, he was forced to reassess his career after losing his job. In facing a career change, he found the courage and motivation to change his unsatisfactory marriage, which was what really needed to happen.

The role Uranus plays, then, is sporadic according to our need for change. Uranus' placement and aspects give us a clue to where that change will take place and how it will unfold. Numerous Uranus aspects, or even just one conjunction that includes a personal planet, indicate that change will be a significant feature in that person's life, resulting in profound growth. As we have seen, transits to these aspects not only bring about changes pertaining to the planets and houses involved, but to other areas as well.

Uranus Aspects That Represent Patterns from the Past

Uranus squares, oppositions, and some conjunctions may represent patterns from the past; however, the soft aspects never do. The hard aspects to Uranus point to impulsive, impatient, and rash behavior in former lifetimes. If such a pattern exists, these tendencies are likely to be reiterated in the signs or chart themes. Knowing this can help you determine if an aspect represents a pattern from a past life or if it was chosen to balance too much conservatism and restraint. Oddly enough, those inclined toward rash behavior are likely to have fire signs, a prominent Uranus, or several Uranus squares because patience and self-control are best learned through negative consequences. By acting out their impulsiveness and impatience, they attract experiences that teach them to slow down and be more careful. Let's look at some examples to see how Uranus aspects portraying past patterns originate.

In Kurt's chart, Saturn and Uranus in Capricorn are conjunct in the fifth house and square Mercury in the second house. This configuration represents his accidental death while rock climbing in a former lifetime. Kurt's daring was first rewarded many lifetimes before this accident when he successfully saved several people from a mountain snowstorm. After that, he continued to look for ways to exceed the normal limits of human endurance. Repeated successes reinforced his daring spirit, which is represented in his current chart by Uranus square Mercury. At some point, his daring was bound to catch up to him. Saturn in Capricorn in the fifth house represents Kurt's tragic mountain death and its residual fear, which now tempers his earlier impetuousness with caution and practicality. Saturn reflects the new attitude he will bring to his recreational activities (fifth house). His soul's intent is that he will overcome any fear that remains and remember to be more cautious.

Bruce has worked hard to establish himself in business. His twenties and thirties were fast-paced and exciting. Relationships, however, eluded him. Usually, he was too preoccupied with work to invest time and energy in them, but more is behind his behavior. Bruce has a square between Mars and Uranus in the fourth and seventh houses, which represents his need for an independent and unusual personal life. This square has served him well by providing him with the courage, drive, and determination to succeed, while divorcing him from the realm of family and relationships long enough to launch his career. This aspect also has a past-life history.

In a former lifetime, he came to a cliff while skiing but stayed safely away. A friend saw him there and, not seeing the cliff, skied right over it to his death. This tragedy deeply affected Bruce. However, instead of increasing his fear of life, as it might have (which might appear in a future chart as a Saturn square), it increased his determination to live life courageously. This attitude is reflected in his Uranus/Mars square. This same square has been in many of his previous charts, which is undoubtedly why he reacted as he did.

Today, Bruce's courage and daring are being used in his life task, which is common. Aspects that represent past patterns are often used in the life task, particularly aspects with Uranus and Neptune. Hard Uranus and Neptune aspects often represent gifts of a sort, though they may have been misapplied at times.

This story also illustrates that aspects do not always continue working throughout life or continue working the same way. Their effects change according to our needs and maturity. Bruce's Uranus/Mars square is no longer needed to advance his career, and he will soon marry.

One final point: Bruce's daring has yet to bring about a tragedy. How someone handles the urge for adventure and whether it ends in tragedy depends on his or her development and the remainder of the chart. If someone becomes attracted to defying death early in his evolution, tragedy is likely because we lack judgment in those early lifetimes.

Uranus Aspects That Supply a Needed Energy

Both hard and soft aspects to Uranus may serve to supply a needed energy. The last example showed how a square supplied the independence and drive to launch a demanding career in addition to representing a past pattern. The next story is another example of how even challenging Uranus aspects can be helpful.

Alan has an earthy chart. Not surprisingly, he is an employer's dream: responsible, hardworking, and efficient. These qualities are his gifts, and they are useful to his life task, just as they have been in former lifetimes. Although his earthy gifts need no improvement, Alan needs more than just work in his life to be well-rounded. Uranus in his fifth house trine his Ascendant was chosen to help him break loose from his conservatism, at least during his leisure hours. Because trines to the Ascendant are the only trines that do not have to be earned, they may be used to supply an energy, as in this case. This placement allows Alan to experience a wilder side of himself during off-hours and to relieve the tension of his long working hours. Another aspect, Uranus square Mercury, adds originality to his thinking and draws other unusual people to him, along with a little more excitement.

Uranus aspects add uniqueness, originality, inventiveness, intuition, and individualism to a chart when they are operating favorably. When they are not, they add impetuousness, rebelliousness, impatience, and willfulness. The negative qualities of Uranus (or Aquarius) become refined over many lifetimes and evolve into positive qualities. However, not all other energies evolve this way. For instance, the strengths of Saturn do not *evolve* from Saturn's pessimism, fear, and discouragement, but are developed by *overcoming* them. Understanding how each of the energies evolves can help us determine, very generally, someone's level of development.

The number of Uranus aspects in a chart indicates the importance of this energy for good or for ill. Numerous Uranus aspects, unless they are all harmonious, may indicate a deep-seated problem. On the other hand, numerous Uranus aspects, including some challenging ones, may also indicate remarkable gifts. Generalizations about the meaning of these aspects are difficult to make. We have to look at the whole chart and rely on intuition to understand each instance.

Neptune Aspects

With Neptune, as with Uranus, the hard and soft aspects are not very different from each other. Depending on the remainder of the chart and the individual's development, challenging Neptune aspects are as likely to represent talents or positive qualities as not, though generally the talents will not be as developed as those represented by trines. Like Uranus, Neptune's negative qualities evolve into positive ones. However, this is where the similarity ends.

Neptune aspects stimulate our desire for God and help us cope with the suffering inherent in being human through the intuition and spiritual attunement they grant. They are a spiritualizing force, drawing us away from mundane activities into the realm of intuition and spirit. How these aspects affect us depends on our development, however. In the chart of someone less advanced, they contribute to escapism and avoiding responsibilities, which is why they are rarely chosen by very young souls. In the chart of a young soul, they usually symbolize a failure to deal with reality in past lives. When this is the case, the remainder of the chart is chosen to strengthen the ego. In the chart of someone more advanced, Neptune aspects promote selfless service, ego-transcendence, and mysticism. Somewhere in between these two extremes, Neptune aspects stimulate creativity and musical expression, which bridge the gap between the mundane and the spiritual.

Neptune Aspects That Represent Patterns from the Past

Just as hard aspects to Uranus might represent negative patterns from the past (as well as gifts), so might hard aspects to Neptune, although soft ones never do. The following examples illustrate how a hard Neptune aspect might originate.

Meg's chart has strong Piscean and Cancer themes. With this much water, either watery gifts or watery challenges are likely. Meg is a highly gifted psychic who channels energy for healing. In her chart, Neptune is conjunct the Sun, sextile the Moon, and trine the Midheaven—all harmonious aspects. However, a square from Neptune in the sixth house to Mars in the third house reflects an instance of abusing her psychic powers in a former lifetime. Before she was tempted to repeat this mistake, a balancing took place, also represented by this aspect. The lesson, which was both painful and eye-opening, brought her a new understanding about power.

Nancy's chart is earthy, although she has a prominent Neptune, which is square her Sun and Moon. This T-Square represents her loss of identity and home when she was forced into a convent in a former lifetime. She never accepted her fate then, and died unhappy and alone. Unlike the former example, this configuration does not represent an attitude that needed to be dissolved, but an incident that affected Nancy's psyche. As a result, Nancy now rejects all religion and belief in God. She learned the value of freedom, but she also became cynical and fatalistic. Her sense of powerlessness and fatalism is pervasive now, and her earthy chart doesn't help. We have to wonder why her soul chose a chart that fosters fatalism rather than balances it. The earthy chart is appropriate now, however, because her life task is fighting for freedom from religion. Nancy's work with an organization is helping to advance this freedom, while healing her old psychological wound. Since she was unable to take action in her own behalf in a former lifetime, doing that now is empowering and healing for her.

Catherine is working as a psychotherapist in an alcohol and drug rehabilitation program. Part of her job is helping people understand why they became substance abusers. Many turn to drugs to fulfill a spiritual longing or emptiness, which is why the Twelve Step program of Alcoholics Anonymous is so successful. In her last lifetime, Catherine coped with the memories of a difficult childhood by taking a drug that made her feel good temporarily. When the drug wore off, she took more to numb her feelings. This former negative relationship with her feelings is represented in Catherine's chart by a square between Neptune and the Moon. Nevertheless, that lifetime was not totally lost to substance abuse. At one point, she realized how debilitating her habit was and tried to overcome it. Although she did not succeed then, the pain of her addiction created a soul-drive to help drug addicts in this lifetime. If she had not made so much progress then, she might have repeated the old pattern today instead of becoming a substance abuse counselor.

As this story shows, it is impossible to tell from the chart alone to what degree a pattern is operating, or if it is operating at all. An aspect may merely represent a negative behavior from the past from which we have learned, as it did in this case. Catherine's Neptune/Moon square reflects her former addiction while fueling her current spiritual search, as do most Neptune aspects.

Neptune Aspects That Supply a Needed Energy

Neptune aspects represent our level of attunement to the energy of Neptune. The soft aspects—the trines, sextiles, and harmonious conjunctions—represent some degree of mastery of Neptune's gifts and lessons. The challenging aspects may also represent similar, but lesser, accomplishments. Both soft and hard aspects to Neptune may be used to add more compassion, sensitivity, intuition, empathy, selflessness, or spiritual understanding to the chart. However, the hard aspects usually do not provide as high an expression of these qualities as the trines. The next example shows how a Neptune aspect might be used to supply energy for the life task.

Craig's life task involves helping primates that are near extinction. He has spent many years studying their habits and behaviors. Because of the work he does, he is not used to being with people. However, he enjoys spending time alone because he is so introspective and attuned to nature. These characteristics are represented by Neptune trine his Sun in the sixth house, and by the Piscean theme in his chart. He has spent many lifetimes developing his compassion and sensitivity to animals. This lifetime is a continuation of similar life tasks in former lifetimes. Because he has spent more lifetimes with Pisces than with any other sign, he is very comfortable with it. However, because he lacks experience with certain other signs, he finds some areas of life difficult, particularly relationships. Apparently, since his soul chose a chart that showcases his Piscean gifts without requiring him to be involved in relationships, facing this imbalance in his development is not important yet. Undoubtedly, the time will come in his evolution when he will have to acquire the missing skills. Then, the chart may reflect his Piscean gifts only minimally.

Pluto Aspects

Hard aspects to Pluto often describe an experience in a former lifetime of loss that profoundly affects the psyche. Like hard aspects to Saturn, hard aspects to Pluto describe a past-life event that needs balancing or healing more often than they supply a needed energy or represent a gift. The opposite is true for hard Uranus and Neptune aspects. Even when they do relate to an incident from the past, they usually don't describe the incident through the signs, houses, and planets, like hard Saturn and Pluto aspects do, but rather the result of the incident. However, hard aspects to Pluto are not always challenging, since they may also represent gifts or positive attributes. Gifts represented by hard aspects, however, are likely to be less developed and more difficult to tap than those represented by trines. Trines may reflect gifts at the level of genius, but squares never do.

Hard Aspects to Pluto That Represent Patterns from the Past

Pluto squares involving a personal planet are the aspects most likely to describe significant loss in the past. However, when a conjunction involving a personal planet serves this purpose, which it does infrequently, the event's impact is likely to be particularly great. Issues or events symbolized by an opposition are usually secondary; their lessons are often learned through others, and possibly just by observing someone else struggling with the issues represented by the aspected planet.

Because squares between Saturn or Pluto and the personal planets often represent our biggest challenges and psychological issues, they should be carefully examined intuitively to determine their meaning. If they do describe a past-life incident, the underlying issue is likely to be a significant one. This is why these aspects should be studied—not because the details of a past-life event are important. Usually, the past-life event described by this kind of Pluto square is the loss or death of a loved one. Pluto and Saturn both represent death, but in different ways. Hard aspects to Pluto represent a transformation of attitudes, beliefs, feelings, ideas, or approaches, with personal loss acting as a catalyst. Hard aspects to Saturn more often symbolize an actual death in a former lifetime, which has crystallized into a fear. This is an important distinction.

With Saturn, the fear needs to be overcome. With Pluto, the transformative work needs to continue. The soul will bring whatever is necessary to continue the transformation, which could even include further loss. Thus, hard aspects to Pluto often symbolize a stage in psychological transformation, which could manifest as more loss or as special insight resulting from a former loss.

Pluto teaches its lessons through loss. The pain of loss teaches us the joy of love by contrasting it to life without someone we love. In this way, loss is bittersweet, reminding us of the depth of our love and our need for one another. As a result, we are more willing to share and cooperate with others. Thus, Pluto and its lessons of love and loss teach us about trust, intimacy, sharing, cooperation, and letting go.

Matthew is suffering from possessiveness. This is common in the charts of those with a strong Scorpio theme or with significant or numerous Pluto aspects. His story should help explain why this is often the case. Matthew's possessiveness is represented by Pluto square Venus, a difficult aspect in any chart when it represents a past-life event. In Matthew's chart, this aspect symbolizes his wife's betrayal in a former lifetime. He responded to his shame and grief then by shutting himself off from others, dying alone and bitter. Today, Matthew is coping with the effects of this by trying to control his lover, which may well result in the very loss he so fears. With Venus in Leo in the fifth house, Matthew will have plenty of opportunities for romance and for learning this lesson, represented by this fifth house/eighth house square. Aspects involving the fifth and eighth houses should always be examined for possible themes pertaining to lost love. This difficult lesson is usually reflected in these houses.

Pluto squares also often represent willful or oppressive attitudes and opinions, as shown in the next example. Brent has Pluto in Leo in the sixth house square Mercury in Taurus in the third house, which represents the loss of his tongue in a bizarre accident in a former lifetime. As a result of being mute, he was ostracized and isolated for the rest of that lifetime. In reaction to this former experience of frustrated communication, Brent now expresses himself vehemently about everything, in keeping with the traditional interpretation of Pluto square Mercury.

Andrew experienced a particularly painful event in his childhood in a former lifetime, marring his ability to form close relationships then and now. This is represented by Pluto in Virgo in the fourth house square the Moon in Sagittarius in the seventh house. Pluto in the fourth house symbolizes a cataclysm in a former lifetime in which he lost his entire family. This affected his emotional well-being and sense of self (the Moon), which cut to the core of his being. The emotional damage from that lifetime lingers into the present one. He remains guarded with his feelings and moves through life with a sense of impending disaster. Tragic experiences leave an intensity and depth of emotion on an unconscious level, which can linger for lifetimes. As a result, many with Pluto squares or difficult conjunctions appear serious and self-absorbed.

Andrew is likely to be able to overcome these feelings because the remainder of his chart was chosen to do that. Jupiter conjunct his Ascendant, and the Moon in Sagittarius, add confidence and an outgoing personality. His Sun in Libra also encourages involvement with others. These chart factors make it likely he will find the help he needs to understand his feelings. This aspect, Pluto square Moon, has the potential for becoming an asset once Andrew overcomes his own psychological barriers to peace and happiness. Aspects like these are often responsible for our greatest strengths because overcoming our difficulties equips us to help others with theirs. Through the trials of Pluto, we gain inner strength and understanding.

Hard Aspects to Pluto That Supply a Needed Energy

When Scorpio energy is needed in a chart, hard aspects to Pluto may be used to supply it. The qualities supplied by these aspects are metaphysical and psychological understanding, concentration, determination, and emotional intensity. If someone is very airy, these aspects provide depth and emotional understanding, which balance the superficiality and intellectuality of air. If someone is too earthbound and practical, they supply the drive to understand life's deeper mysteries. If someone needs endurance or determination to complete the life task, they supply these qualities as well. The examples that follow show how hard aspects to Pluto may be used to supply energy.

Greg has trouble asserting himself in his career and relationships because he is afraid of offending others. In former lifetimes, his tendency has been to let others make choices for him. Greg's chart has several factors designed to counteract this tendency: Pluto square Mars, an Aries Ascendant, and the Moon in the fifth house in Leo. Pluto square Mars adds forcefulness and determination if someone lacks these qualities, as in this case. Now when Greg displays assertiveness, we don't know whether it is coming from his Aries Ascendant, his Leo Moon, this Pluto aspect, or another chart factor. When aspects are supplying a certain energy, their effects are not great, and other chart factors will be serving a similar function.

Phil has fought many illnesses throughout his life and is now fighting AIDS. His lengthy history of illness, including AIDS, was a pre-life choice to accelerate his evolution. We are free to make a choice like this if it is felt we have the development to handle it successfully or, at least, to learn from it. So far, Phil has been able to cope with the challenges of illness. It remains to be seen how he will handle the ultimate challenge—death. It is part of Phil's work to help bring about a new understanding about death through his own acceptance of it. Like Phil, many people dying now have chosen to set an example for others about death and dying so that in the future a new attitude about death can emerge. This is one way that AIDS is being used by the souls of those who have chosen it. Most diseases like AIDS are chosen before life to serve some purpose in our growth or in humanity's Plan.

Since Pluto pertains to transformation, it is fitting that it rules death as well—the ultimate transformation. To facilitate Phil's Plan, his chart has many hard and soft aspects to Pluto, making it likely that he will be able to tap the transformative power of Pluto. He has managed to transform something about himself—an attitude, a habit, a perception—with each of his illnesses. Without the illnesses to challenge him, he is not as likely to have made these changes. Pluto square Mercury and the Moon in Phil's sixth house represent the illnesses that have led and will lead to his transformation and death. Pluto square the Moon symbolizes the impact of these illnesses on his emotional self, which will be forever changed, and on his family members, who are being transformed along with him. Pluto square Mercury symbolizes the effect of these illnesses on his view of life and death. He may even write or give speeches about what he has learned or share his journey with others some other way. Although this is not a typical example of hard aspects to Pluto that supply energy, it is a variation, since the aspects were chosen, rather than required, and serve his life task.

Soft Aspects to Pluto

Harmonious Pluto aspects, particularly the trines and some conjunctions, indicate gifts gained by mastering Pluto's lessons. The lessons, as we have seen, usually involve loss of some sort and teach us to love, share, cooperate, trust, and let go. In our early lifetimes, love is confused with lust, ownership, dependency, and power. As we evolve, our ability to love becomes purified. Many lifetimes of intimacy and sharing are needed to effect this transformation. Pluto's lessons teach us to love more purely. Those with harmonious Pluto aspects, particularly the trines, have demonstrated a level of love that is not possessive, dependent, and controlling. However, as with all trines, that level will not be discernible from the chart. Some trines indicate only minor gifts, while others, like in the next example, indicate great gifts.

Kristin has Pluto conjunct her Sun in Leo and trine her Moon in Sagittarius. This indicates a gift for self-transformation, which she now applies in her work as a psychotherapist. These aspects reflect the insight she has acquired in previous lifetimes through experiences with loss and intimacy. As a result, she is equipped to help others understand themselves and their relationships. With Pluto trine her Moon, she is an expert in understanding emotions and helping others with emotional issues.

When a Pluto aspect represents a gift, it represents one of the more valuable ones. The ability to transform oneself, utilize change positively, and see the good in a crisis are especially valuable because life is about change, growth, and transformation. Pluto trines indicate an ability to approach life's challenges with acceptance, understanding, and courage, and without the need to control and manipulate life, as with Pluto squares.

A DEEPER LOOK AT ASPECT ANALYSIS

Every aspect is contained within signs and houses, which further delineate it. An aspect's planets and signs describe an internal conflict, a gift, or an event in a past life or the present one, that has had or will have a psychological impact. The houses involved in an aspect describe the areas of life likely to be most affected by this internal conflict, gift, or event. This section will look more closely at how the aspects, houses, and signs depict these various psychological complexes, gifts, and events.

Aspects that Describe Psychological Complexes

The aspects that describe psychological complexes are most often the squares, sometimes the oppositions and conjunctions, and occasionally the trines or sextiles. If a trine or sextile represents an issue, it is only a mild one or operates negatively only occasionally. Squares are most representative of our psychological issues, at least those most resistant to change. Oppositions are most apparent in our relationships and often represent an internal conflict that is experienced through others. Conjunctions may represent a primary psychological trait for good or for bad. The conjunctions that describe psychological complexes are usually ones that involve antagonistic groupings of one or more of the outer planets (Saturn, Uranus, Neptune, and Pluto) with the personal planets, especially the Sun, the Moon, and Mars. Many psychological issues that are represented by hard aspects involve an internal conflict whose sides are depicted by the planets, signs, and houses. The examples that follow illustrate some of these conflicts.

Melissa has two sides of herself that compete for her time and attention. One side is driven to pursue self-development through a career, and the other is driven to fulfill herself through personal relationships. She feels guilty because she doesn't feel that she does justice to either need. The aspect symbolizing this internal conflict is Mars in Libra square her Capricorn Sun. The conflict between self-development and involvement with others is one of the most common internal conflicts. It may also be symbolized in aspects between the following pairs of signs: Libra/Aries, Cancer/Capricorn, Scorpio/Taurus, and Cancer/Aries. People generally need to find a balance between self-development and their relationships. Unless a life task demands one kind of development over the other, this conflict is usually present. This is one way that the soul ensures even development.

The second example involves an issue that is not as common or as easily resolved. It is represented in David's chart by Saturn and Mercury in Aries square Mars in Capricorn. David's energy (Mars) is being restricted and contained by Saturn, and this same conflict is mirrored in the signs. Unlike Aries, Capricorn is cautious, premeditated, and practical. This creates a push-pull effect within David, as if he has one foot on the accelerator and one on the brake. David is unable to get out of bed in the morning and face his responsibilities. He has no energy to deal with daily concerns, much less long-term goals. This conflict may also be symbolized in aspects between the following pairs of signs: Aries/Cancer,

Leo/Pisces, Sagittarius/Cancer, Aries/Virgo, and Sagittarius/Taurus. The energies in these pairs often cancel each other out rather than allow for alternating expression. When this happens, the person becomes stalemated, making goals hard to achieve. Sometimes, an aspect like this is used to balance a past-life tendency to be either too impetuous or too cautious. When that is the case, it is not as hard to handle. However, these aspects are more likely to represent a similar pattern in the past of blocked energy. In that case, the remainder of the chart will have signs that encourage one side of the conflict over the other to break the stalemate.

One of the hardest internal conflicts is between introversion and extroversion. Until this conflict is integrated, people feel untrue to themselves no matter what they do. When they express themselves, they feel that they have betrayed their privacy. When they withhold themselves, they feel unhappy and dissatisfied with how they think others perceive them. This conflict also may be symbolized in aspects between the following pairs of signs: Aries/Cancer, Aries/Capricorn, Aries/Virgo, Aries/Taurus, Aries/Scorpio, Leo/Capricorn, Leo/Taurus, Leo/Pisces, Leo/Scorpio, Sagittarius/Cancer, Sagittarius/Virgo, Sagittarius/Pisces, or Sagittarius/Taurus. Any combination of fire with water or earth signifies this conflict.

The planets may represent an internal conflict as well as the signs. Some planets by nature are opposite, such as Mars and Venus, the Sun and the Moon, and Saturn and Jupiter. Aspects involving planets that are opposite in nature increase the potential conflict indicated by the aspect or the signs. Mars, in particular, included in an aspect increases its intensity and challenge. On the other hand, Venus and Jupiter often dull or cancel the conflict in aspects in which they are found. Mercury's adaptability and neutrality make Mercury aspects milder also.

The houses may also represent an internal conflict. The opposition aspect connects areas of life that are opposing but potentially complementary. The houses that present the most likelihood of conflict when involved in aspects are the tenth and fourth, the first and seventh, the second and eighth, and squares between the

seventh and tenth, and the first and fourth. These houses represent the most basic human conflict: self versus others. When the
houses, signs, and planets all describe the same conflict, it will be
deeper than if each describes a different conflict. The examples
that follow illustrate some more common conflicts.

Patricia has a Grand Cross in cardinal signs in the mutable
houses. The Cardinal Grand Cross represents the conflict between
self and others. Its placement in the mutable houses indicates that
this conflict will play itself out in the realm of ideas and ideals.
Patricia will have a need for both independence and relationship,
and she will want to understand this conflict. She may study this
dilemma to try to understand it and integrate these two aspects of
her life. She may even become an expert in balancing these two
areas of life and teach others how to do so.

Carl is an example of the opposite situation. Carl has a Grand
Cross in mutable signs in the cardinal houses. The Mutable
Grand Cross represents a need to understand life. Because it is in
the cardinal houses, he will gain this understanding through cardinal house matters: home, family, relationships, and self-development. Planets in the cardinal houses demand that we balance
these different areas of life, which is no small task. Through this
balancing act, Carl will gain a better understanding of how he can
lead a more fulfilling and meaningful life.

Aspects that Describe Events

Sometimes aspects describe an event related to the planets, signs,
and houses involved. Events are usually portrayed in aspects other
than the trines or sextiles. The examples that follow show how
aspects that describe events operate in the chart.

Nick has cancer. This disease was chosen by him before life as a
means for growth, and is symbolized by Mars conjunct Pluto in his
sixth house. Contrary to what we might think, this aspect does not
manifest as belligerence or difficulty working with others, nor does
it mean Nick committed an abuse in a former lifetime that he is
paying for with ill health. It means that death (Pluto) is imminent
from an aggressive (Mars) disease, and that is all. This aspect has

had no other effect or meaning in his life; it has remained mute until now. Some aspects, like this one, are inexplicable during much of our lives. Let's look at another example.

Hank was a hardworking, security-minded insurance salesperson who died suddenly in an automobile accident. In providing his family with life insurance, he acted out of an unconscious knowledge of his own death. Hank's chart has an inconjunct between Mars, Pluto, and Uranus in the third and eighth houses, indicating his sudden and violent death. Inconjuncts describe an incident in a former lifetime that is being faced and balanced in the current one. This was true for Hank, too, though it also represented a current event, as aspects sometimes do.

When balancing an experience from the past depends on a repetition or near repetition of that experience, aspects often represent both a past event and a present one. Hank lost his life in a boating collision in a former lifetime, which brought him a new awareness about life during his afterlife experience. As a result, he chose to repeat this experience as a way of continuing his examination of sudden death. Next, is an example that does not involve a tragedy.

Jason attends high school with his brother, Scott, who is one year behind him. Scott has made a pre-life agreement to help Jason meet the woman he is likely to marry. This agreement is represented in Jason's chart by a third house conjunction of Venus and Mercury. Venus, the planet of love and relationship, is in the house that rules siblings and early education, and conjunct the natural ruler (Mercury) of this house. This is a simple example, but many of the aspects in this category are equally simple and do not represent tragic events. Like all aspects, those that describe events manifest in varying degrees.

Aspects that Describe Gifts

Gifts are described by trines, some conjunctions, and to a lesser extent, sextiles, which represent gifts in the making. Oppositions and squares may also represent gifts once they become integrated, but this takes work and, often, the better part of a lifetime.

Marsha's musical gifts are reflected in a Grand Trine in air. The planets involved in her Grand Trine are Mercury in Aquarius (dexterity and inspiration), Mars in Gemini (drive and more dexterity), and the Moon in Libra (sensitivity and appreciation of music). Taken together, these provide the basic ingredients for musicianship. Marsha has honed her musical skills in several other lifetimes, with technique being her greatest strength. Had her forte been emotional expression, her Grand Trine would probably have been in water rather than air. Not surprisingly, the music Marsha most enjoys is light and airy—like Mozart's. He had the Sun, Venus, Mercury, and Saturn in Aquarius, and Uranus on an angle.

Herb also has a Grand Trine in air, but it reflects a different gift. He is a research scientist who is looking for a cure for cancer. Herb's Grand Trine falls in the fire houses and involves Uranus, the Moon, and Mars. This combination of fire and air is potent in providing mental inspiration and new ideas. Uranus in Gemini provides mental inspiration, Mars in Libra gives drive and cooperative effort, and the Moon in Aquarius gives intuition. This Grand Trine, although not a watery one, is highly creative.

Marvin has another type of airy gift. He is well respected in the electronics field and has excellent organizational abilities. His Grand Trine in air in the earth houses lends practicality to his mental abilities. Saturn in Gemini in his second house adds business acumen, organizational ability, thoroughness, and practicality. Mercury in Aquarius in his tenth house contributes further to intellectuality, practical know-how, and motivation to achieve in an electronics career.

As you can see, every Grand Trine (or trine) describes skills that were developed in former lifetimes, but ones that cannot be determined from the chart alone.

CHAPTER 5

THE
MOON

The Moon in the birth chart helps us understand the impact our early environment has had on our psychology. It describes the early environment that was chosen for this lifetime and the emotional style, which results from the environment. The early environment is important because it conditions our responses. It shapes how we instinctively respond to life and how we deal with our emotions.

Just as we must experience the styles and lessons of the twelve Sun signs as part of our evolution, we must experience the styles and lessons of the twelve Moon signs. Each of the twelve styles is unique and serves a purpose. Secondary purposes may be to aid the life task and balance a karmic debt, but the Moon sign is primarily chosen to experience life through that sign's emotional style. This variety of perception allows souls a multiplicity of experiences from which to glean understanding.

The emotions are a significant part of being human. They inform us of our physical, emotional, intellectual, and spiritual needs. Without the information that our emotions provide, we could not identify our needs, and needs that are not identified may not be met. Each Moon sign differs in its awareness of its needs and its approach to meeting them. As a result, some styles are more conducive to healthy emotional functioning than others. The signs that deal less effectively with emotions will meet with lessons, which will result in growth. That is the purpose of these signs. Life is about learning and growing. To accomplish this, we must be exposed to all kinds of human experience. Nevertheless, though some Moon signs are more conducive to healthy emotional functioning than others, no Moon sign is entirely favorable or unfavorable. Each Moon sign offers a variety of possible experiences. Whether we experience a Moon sign as difficult or not depends on a number things, especially the purpose for choosing that sign.

THE TWELVE EMOTIONAL STYLES

Aries Moon

Aries Moons are focused on their needs and demand that others meet them, while eschewing any dependence on others. They give the appearance of not needing anyone and are, indeed, more self-sufficient than most. They are adept at taking care of their own needs. Their relationships with others tend to be adversarial and competitive, which makes this Moon sign challenging in intimate relationships. Another reason this is potentially one of the more difficult placements for the Moon is that the expressiveness of Mars is incongruous with the retentiveness of the Moon. The tendency with Moon in Aries is to express the emotions, which are mostly inexpressible. How easy it is, then, to express them poorly, especially since Aries may not have the patience to do it carefully and properly.

It's not that Aries Moons have more feelings; they just express them more freely. This is an important distinction because some Moon signs do have a deeper emotional nature than others. Aries is not one of them. Nevertheless, Aries Moons express the feelings they do have and often do it rashly and without thought. This usually results in misplaced, projected, or disowned feelings. Aries Moons let their feelings go unchecked, and feelings that go unchecked and unanalyzed may be twisted into blame by the ego for self-protection. Because Aries Moons often blame others for their feelings, their outstanding emotion is anger. The cure is for them to slow down and examine their feelings honestly before expressing them. Once they have learned to do this, they can be adept at getting their needs met. Then, their emotions can function as a tool rather than a weapon.

On a more positive note, this Moon sign may be chosen to balance a more retentive personality or chart. When this is the case, it will operate favorably, giving the individual the impetus to express himself in a healthy way when otherwise he might not have expressed himself at all. The gift of this Moon sign is emotional self-sufficiency and an ability to nurture themselves by going after what they need.

Taurus Moon

This Moon sign is fixed, and has difficulty letting go of negative emotions and moving on emotionally. Forgiveness is not a strong point of Taurus Moons. Like Scorpio Moons, Taurus Moons harbor grudges for a long time. Repression of emotions is common. This is easily understood when we realize that earth muffles and hides water, the emotional element. The elements behave as might be expected: air feeds fire, earth stifles fire, water extinguishes fire, and earth absorbs water. "Absorb" is the key word here. Earth signs do not experience their emotions as much as other signs do. Their emotions are absorbed as they arise, leaving little opportunity for them to be acknowledged and acted upon. They disappear into the unconscious where they are dealt with by other means, such as through dreams and by enduring. Taurus has the capacity to endure, and Taurus Moons endure emotions. Rather than using emotions as messages about their needs, Taurus Moons may ignore their needs and "grin and bear it." This strategy is useful when we are powerless to do anything about getting our needs met. However, Taurus Moons may let even the needs that can be met go unmet, which can result in unfulfilled potentials or even a misguided life. Because they don't know how they feel, they often let other people's feelings overrule their own. Then, they might find themselves living out someone else's dreams rather than their own. This is the tragedy of those who are unaware of their emotions and don't assert themselves to get their needs met.

Taurus Moons have to learn to feel their feelings, and then they have to value them enough to do something about the needs they represent. Taurus Moons also get into trouble by not making the changes that are necessary for their growth and expansion because change, especially anything that involves their home or emotional life, is an anathema to them. Because they resist even positive change, they get stuck in ruts and suffer more than they have to.

Gemini Moon

Gemini Moons are not known for their emotional constancy. This is a mutable sign, and the Moon in a mutable sign is especially changeable. They may feel one way one minute and another way the next. The positive side of this is that Gemini Moons don't hold on to anger or other negative feelings for long. They are easygoing and lighthearted. They do like variety in their emotional life, though, and have a reputation for being fickle and playing the field. They have difficulty settling down with one partner because they are curious about other possibilities. To them, variety is truly the spice of life. This Moon sign has its benefits. The rationality and objectivity of Gemini nicely balance the Moon's emotionality. Gemini Moons relish analyzing and discussing feelings. They are curious about their feelings and try to understand them when they arise. They do not necessarily try to feel them, but they do observe them and talk about them.

Gemini Moons are not afraid to look at their feelings because they have the objectivity to not be overcome by them. To them, emotions do not hold power as much as interest. Gemini Moons need to learn what to do with their emotions once they have observed them, however. Their emotions don't impel them to take action like some of the other Moon signs. Gemini Moons tend to get stuck on the mental plane. Their saving grace is that they naturally seek answers to questions about their emotions. Many do learn how to deal with their emotions in a healthy way. Consequently, this can be an ideal placement for teachers of young children, psychotherapists, and others who are in a position to educate others about emotions. On the other hand, some Gemini Moons are cut off from their emotions and disregard them altogether by rationalizing them away. Even those who use their Gemini Moon to analyze their emotions may do this sometimes. When the intellect is used this way, a Gemini Moon becomes a disadvantage.

Cancer Moon

More than any Moon sign, Cancer Moons are at home with their feelings. Feeling feelings is what they do best. They may not understand them or be able to put them into words like Gemini Moons, but they relish every one of them. To them, life is about feeling. The drawback is that they lack objectivity and are easily overcome by their emotions. Cancer Moons are very sensitive and vulnerable to being hurt, and have a strong need for emotional nourishment from others. They can be needy, clinging, possessive, dependent, and demanding of others. On the other hand, their sensitivity and deep compassion for the pain of others make them excellent caregivers. They need to nurture others as much as they need to be nurtured. They are capable of great feats of giving and a depth of loving that few other signs experience. It is because they can feel other people's feelings that Cancer Moons are such fine nurturers.

Not only are Cancer Moons nurturers, many are highly intuitive or psychic. They pay a price for this gift, however, which is that they are easily drained by other people's feelings and needs. When they see a need, they rush to fill it. Their own identity often becomes lost in others and in their role as a nurturer. Cancer Moons are psychic sponges and tend to absorb the emotions of others. This is one reason they are so moody. Their moods fluctuate with the Moon, but also with the moods of others.

Leo Moon

Leo Moons need to feel special. They crave attention and admiration, which often causes them to appear to be vain and proud. Being in love is very important to them because it makes them feel special and unique, and it gives them the attention they crave. Nevertheless, they are very loyal emotionally, since Leo is a fixed sign. This Moon sign is big-hearted, expressive, confident, affectionate, generous, and gregarious, and therefore very likable. Leo Moons are natural entertainers and actors because their feelings are so easily and comfortably expressed. However, like Aries Moons, they are apt to get into trouble with others over how they express their feelings, but for a different reason. They express them in a way that demands attention and acknowledgment of their rightness, as if to say, "I feel it, so it must be right." This creates problems with others, who may not have similar needs and feelings. By being so imperious, they stand to alienate even those who agree with them.

Emotions are neither right nor wrong any more than needs are—they just are. This is what Leo Moons need to learn. They need to learn that although their emotions are valid and valuable, they are not the only ones on the block. Once Leo Moons learn to consider the feelings of others, their own feelings are more readily acknowledged by others.

Virgo Moon

As with a Taurus Moon, a Virgo Moon's emotions are often muffled or absorbed before they are even known; or, like Gemini Moons, Virgo Moons might rationalize their feelings away.

Therefore, they appear cool and standoffish. They don't lack kindness, but they often suffer under this impression, and end up feeling alienated and alone. Like Capricorn Moons, they have a sense of having to go it alone. The difference is that Capricorn Moons don't mind this as much as Virgo Moons do. Virgo Moons feel a lack of connection with others that is painful and often translated into self-blame and self-criticism, and sublimated by working hard. They also have to be careful not to alienate others by being overly critical.

This style serves a purpose, however, in teaching us what it is like to be divorced from the feeling realm. By having a Virgo Moon, we gain an appreciation for the role that feelings play in life. This is an excellent placement for psychotherapists, writers, and others whose work relates to analyzing emotions. Virgo Moons are able to sort through and understand the emotions of others without becoming unduly involved in their emotional dramas. They also are able to understand their own emotions and deal with them coolly and objectively. Their dedication to service is exceptional.

Libra Moon

Libra Moons are pleasing, congenial, sweet, non-confrontational, accommodating, even-tempered, and well-mannered. Because Libra is an air sign, Libra Moons' emotions are not intense, so it is easy for them to express emotions politely and inoffensively. Others who express their emotions more forcefully and freely may offend the sensibilities of a Libra Moon, who feels that displays of emotions are undignified—even scary. Libra Moons handle their emotions with civility and grace, and they are uncomfortable when others don't also. As fond as they are of relationships, they are uncomfortable with whirlwind love affairs and disinclined toward one-night stands. They are loyal, faithful, and conventional in love.

Emotions are not a problem for Libra Moons. They are able to use them to their benefit like no other sign. They are blessed in two ways: with the objectivity common to all airy Moons, and the sweetness of Libra. Their amiability is a real advantage because it helps them get their needs met easily and harmoniously, unless the Moon is afflicted. Because they have a pleasing manner, Libra Moons are popular and easily loved, though not necessarily charismatic. However, their romanticism may interfere with their ability to see others clearly. They often put others on a pedestal, only to be disillusioned when they turn out to be human. This tendency to see the good in others is admirable as long as they are discriminating.

Libra Moons have another problem in relationships: they focus on other people's needs instead of their own. This can leave them unhappy, unfulfilled, and resentful. When they are unhappy, they tend to keep it to themselves because they don't like arguments. As a result, their partner thinks everything is all right when it isn't, and is surprised when the relationship ends without warning. This is why some consider Libra Moons unfeeling. They need to get in touch with their needs and learn to assert themselves.

Scorpio Moon

This is another of the potentially more difficult Moon placements. Scorpio Moons can be sensitive to the point of being morose. They easily slip into negativity and, without other chart factors to uplift them, may find themselves lost in a whirl of negativity and morbid thoughts. Like Taurus Moons, they repress their feelings and hold on to negative ones. These repressed feelings may erupt from time to time into rage. Scorpio Moons also relish drama. They thrive on crisis and emotional upheaval. They don't feel alive unless they are in the grip of intense emotions. They may even create crises just to feel that way. This needs to be overcome. Scorpio Moons need to learn to appreciate life without the emotional intrigue.

Scorpio Moons also need to realize that life is not dependent on their feelings about it. Emotions are part of life, but they aren't everything. Scorpio Moons often become absorbed in the emotional side of life to the exclusion of other aspects. They are intensely passionate and sexual, and they want to merge with and possess their partners.

Another challenge of this placement is expression of feelings. Scorpio Moons have difficulty putting their feelings into words, and they may not even try because they think others couldn't possibly understand them, which isn't true. They also have difficulty trusting others with their feelings, which leaves them feeling alienated and alone. They are very sensitive and afraid of being hurt, so they don't let others know how they feel. Because they keep their feelings to themselves, emotions fester inside them, creating more problems.

On the brighter side, Scorpio Moons have keen psychological insight. They study psychology and the occult in order to understand the forces that move people. Many are psychic as well, and able to be forces for transformation in people's lives once they have transformed their own.

Sagittarius Moon

Sagittarius Moons are fun-loving, optimistic, easygoing, exuberant, adventuresome, and good-natured. They like to "eat, drink, and be merry," and need to watch their tendency to party and overindulge. They are not particularly interested in dealing with their emotions or with the emotional demands of others, and don't easily form close, emotional bonds. Intimacy is not their forte. Freedom is more important to them than closeness or stability, and they are not ones to stay at home. It is not easy for this Moon sign to be faithful because they don't want to limit their experiences by limiting their relationships. What they want most in a partner is someone who can play and go places with them.

Sagittarius Moons especially enjoy the outdoors, sports, and traveling. They may philosophize and joke about their emotions, but more commonly, they deal with them by taking off somewhere. Physical activity and sports are effective ways for them to process their feelings. They need to be physically active to feel good. Nevertheless, their emotions are a secret to no one. Sagittarius Moons are honest and expressive, but, as with all fiery Moons,

166 • *Chapter Five*

the manner in which they express their emotions needs refinement. They lack sensitivity and tact. They blurt out what they feel
and expect others to make concessions for their raw honesty. Con-
fronting them about this can help them to change. Unfortunately,
others are often intimidated by their fiery personality and let them
get away with their inconsiderate and tactless behavior, which only
reinforces it. Once they learn to be more sensitive, they are easy to
like. Their affable and expressive manner is appreciated when it
takes into account the needs and feelings of others.

Capricorn Moon

Capricorn Moons are hardworking, reliable, responsible, dependable, persevering, and restrained. Like the other earth signs, they
have difficulty feeling and expressing their feelings. As a result,
they may appear cold, unfeeling, stiff, controlled, and serious.
They demonstrate their love for others by working hard and sup-
porting them financially, but rarely show any affection. In relationships, they are conservative, loyal, dependable, dutiful, and
persevering. They will persevere in unhappy relationships and jobs
simply out of duty and obligation. They take their responsibilities
very seriously. Because they don't believe that life is easy, they
don't expect it to be. Consequently, they may not even try to
make changes to improve it. They are used to toughing things out
and enduring hardships.

The difficulty Capricorn Moons have with feelings may be the
result of a painful experience in a past life or in this one, which
causes them to be guarded, cautious, and defensive. Their upbringing is often harsh or cold or lacking in the necessities of life. Their
feelings are likely to have been discouraged and their emotional
needs not met, making them feel unlovable. The result is that they
believe that life will not meet their needs even if they ask, so they
conclude, *why ask?* They come to feel that loving only brings them
pain. During our evolution, we must experience everything that is
entailed in having emotions, including the pain of not having our
emotional needs met. This Moon sign teaches us that the result of

withholding our feelings is not only ineffective, but ultimately more painful than expressing them. Capricorn Moons could benefit from psychotherapy, but their self-reliance and reticence do not make it likely that they will seek it out.

Aquarius Moon

Aquarius Moons tend to be independent, willful, stubborn, high-strung, rebellious, unpredictable emotionally, and insensitive to other people's feelings. They value their freedom above all else and are prone to making abrupt changes as a way of demonstrating this. Conventionality and sameness bore them. They are unusual or unconventional in their approach to relationships and sex, and often have unusual associates, though they are loyal to their friends. Their friends are more important to them than romantic liaisons, and their romantic liaisons must also be friends and allow them to have others in their life. They are tolerant of individual differences and enjoy all kinds of people.

The difficulties of this Moon sign stem from a lack of emotional depth and feeling. Aquarius Moons are aloof and detached from their feelings. They are not known for intimacy, which, to them, feels possessive and restrictive of the freedom they value so highly. Although intimacy and emotional depth are not prerequisites to happiness, their absence can create problems in relationships, especially with more emotional types. Aquarius Moons are in touch with a kind of universal love, however, even if one-to-one relationships don't come naturally.

Just as an emotional style that is deep has a purpose, one that lacks depth also has one. An Aquarius Moon allows someone to develop in ways that he otherwise might not have if he were deeply emotional. This style usually develops the intellect or supports an intellectual life task. Even though the emotional side of life is not important to Aquarius Moons, the social side is. Aquarius Moons need involvement with like-minded individuals in activities befitting their ideals. They are idealistic and may be moved to follow a cause in an almost emotional way. Thus, they may not be passionate when it comes to relationships, but their drive for a cause can be quite passionate. Their gifts are tolerance, objectivity, intuition, inventiveness, creativity, and a unique outlook.

Pisces Moon

The Moon functions well in this sign because both the Moon and Pisces are watery. The emotions run deep and change readily, since this is a mutable sign. The advantage of this placement is its sensitivity, compassion, intuition, and devotion. With a Pisces Moon, the feelings are directed toward God, resulting in a highly devotional and religious nature, and a strong need to serve. Pisces Moons are more able than most to experience unconditional love. When they put their sensitivity to good use and are not defeated by it, they are the most loving and affectionate of the Moon signs. Psychic gifts are also a possibility if the individual is developed. Many mystics and mediums have a Pisces Moon, or the Moon in the twelfth house. Its disadvantage is that the emotions may be overwhelming at times unless other chart factors offset this placement, or the individual is evolved.

Pisces Moons are psychic sponges and pick up and react to other people's feelings, including the negative ones. Because of this and their hypersensitivity, they can easily slip into depression, self-pity, or martyrdom. As with the other water signs, their emotions are not easily identified or expressed, and their tendency is to keep them secret. This can be a problem. Unless Pisces Moons learn to express their feelings, they aren't likely to get their needs met. Often, the problem is that they don't value themselves enough to ask for what they want, and they lack the practical know-how to get it themselves. This can result in negativity, resentment, anger, depression, and feeling victimized by life. Because a lack of assertiveness is usually at the bottom of their depression, they need to learn to acknowledge their needs and take steps to get them met.

ASPECTS TO THE MOON

Aspects to the Moon affect its expression. They may either enhance or inhibit the Moon sign's expression. For example, Saturn in hard or soft aspect to a Gemini Moon slows its expression, making it more thoughtful and cautious. Aspects can either reinforce or balance the qualities of the Moon sign. For example, Uranus in aspect to an Aries Moon reinforces its natural impatience, while Saturn balances it by making it more cautious.

Aspects affect the expression of the Moon sign both positively and negatively. The hard aspects are not always a disadvantage because they may perform a balancing function. Besides, hard aspects often operate similarly to soft ones, especially in the charts of those who are developed.

Soft Aspects to the Moon

The soft aspects—trines, sextiles, and harmonious conjunctions—are a positive resource and don't tend to work against us. At worst, they do not act at all. When examining aspects to the Moon, soft aspects should be considered because they can offset the negative effects of the hard ones. Soft aspects to the Moon bring out the positive qualities of the planets and signs involved, and blend them. The positive qualities of the planets and signs will either be enhanced or they will complement each other. For example, Neptune trine a Pisces Moon brings out the best of Pisces, while Neptune trine a Capricorn Moon complements Capricorn with the gentleness and selflessness of Pisces.

Soft aspects represent talents or attributes developed in other lifetimes that are necessary to our work or life task. These gifts may be the result of hard work or of life's daily tests and trials. They are likely to be used in our life task and in overcoming our negative traits. They smooth the way and even neutralize the energy of the more difficult aspects. On the other hand, we often do not appreciate the gifts represented by these aspects, since the abilities they denote come so easily to us. Astrology can help us identify and tap the potential of these talents.

Hard Aspects to the Moon

The hard aspects to the Moon are important because they indicate the difficulties we might encounter in getting our emotional needs met. They represent either blocks in our environment or blocks within ourselves that make getting our emotional needs met difficult. In particular, hard aspects between the Moon and the outer planets—Saturn, Uranus, Neptune, and Pluto—describe these blocks. What follows are descriptions of how the hard aspects between the outer planets and the Moon affect the emotional expression of the Moon signs and, consequently, their ability to get their emotional needs met.

Hard Aspects Between Saturn and the Moon: Hard aspects between *Saturn and an Aries Moon* tone down the impetuousness of Aries. They can be beneficial to an Aries Moon because they slow the individual down long enough for him to gain some insight and control over his emotions.

Hard aspects between *Saturn and a Taurus Moon* reinforce the Taurus Moon's cautiousness and conservatism, making it even harder for the individual to move forward and accept change. These aspects are mainly disadvantageous but, unless they represent an entrenched pattern of inflexibility, were probably chosen for a reason.

Hard aspects between *Saturn and a Gemini Moon* are usually helpful because they discipline its fluidity and adaptability, and limit its curiosity. These aspects may have been chosen either to balance over-adaptability or to provide a challenge, which, when overcome, will result in growth.

Hard aspects between *Saturn and a Cancer Moon* add to its moodiness, pessimism, and depression. These aspects can be quite difficult. However, they may be used to develop strength, aid the life task, or balance a karmic debt or negative pattern from the past.

Hard aspects between *Saturn and a Leo Moon* may blunt its confidence. The Leo Moon might overcompensate for this insecurity by acting all the more arrogantly. Although these individuals feel unsure about expressing themselves, they also feel compelled to, which results in an uncomfortable internal conflict. These aspects may have been chosen to balance a domineering attitude or to temper the exuberance of this Moon sign so that the individual fits more comfortably into non-leadership roles; or, these aspects may have been chosen to add discipline to the Leo Moon's creativity or to develop a specific talent.

Hard aspects between *Saturn and a Virgo Moon* amplify this Moon sign's tendency toward isolation, moroseness, and feelings of inadequacy. These individuals are challenged to love and accept themselves regardless of imperfections or feelings of alienation. These aspects may have been chosen to accelerate growth. They may cause the individual to turn within and find comfort in virtuous qualities already present, or to develop them as a way of increasing self-esteem or gaining the acceptance desired from others.

Hard aspects between *Saturn and a Libra Moon* may cause frustration or delays in relationships. These individuals may find their insecurities interfering with their ability to assert themselves toward getting their emotional needs met. The Libra Moon's need for companionship may be thwarted or blocked by the belief that he is not lovable, which is his greatest fear. These aspects may have been chosen to balance dependency by forcing the individual to be more independent. If that were the case, their purpose would be to build a stronger sense of self. After this is accomplished, a successful partnership is more likely.

Hard aspects between *Saturn and a Scorpio Moon* add pessimism and a need for control and power. As a result, these individuals have difficulty enjoying life, relaxing, and letting down their defenses. They assume everything is of dire consequence to their position in life. Since position is so important to them, they may manipulate and connive to control situations. On the positive side, these individuals may have keen intellects and reasoning powers, excellent insight into human nature, and an ability to do research or detective work.

Hard aspects between *Saturn and a Sagittarius Moon* temper the boisterous and sometimes overly exuberant energy of the

Sagittarius Moon so that it can operate more practically and realistically. Saturn aspects to this Moon bring discipline, realism, caution, patience, and endurance, all qualities that may be lacking in many Sagittarius Moons.

Hard aspects between *Saturn and a Capricorn Moon* reinforce its pessimism and seriousness. Like hard aspects between Saturn and a Virgo Moon, they may have been chosen to accelerate growth.

Hard aspects between *Saturn and an Aquarius Moon*, like these same aspects to a Scorpio Moon, make for an incisive and probing mind. The creativity and inspiration of the Aquarius Moon is disciplined and given some structure by these aspects. They are usually chosen to aid the work or the life task. They add to the already cool and aloof emotional style of the Aquarius Moon, making his energies more available for humanitarian causes or work rather than relationships.

Hard aspects between *Saturn and a Pisces Moon* are more beneficial than not. They give the diffuse and intangible energy of Pisces some structure, realism, and discipline. Saturn offers the qualities that Pisces most lacks: realism, persistence, discipline, patience, and practicality. These aspects are often chosen to balance negative Piscean tendencies from past lives, while maintaining Piscean gifts.

Hard Aspects Between Uranus and the Moon: People with hard aspects between Uranus and the Moon are likely to have chosen them to aid their life task, for they add uniqueness and originality. If, instead, they reflect a pattern of impetuousness, inconsistency, or rudeness developed in former lifetimes, then the individual is likely to be thwarted until patience, steadfastness, and courtesy prevail over this pattern.

Hard aspects between *Uranus and an Aries Moon* aggravate its potential to be impatient, impulsive, and headstrong. On the other hand, they add to its inventiveness, independence, and energy.

Hard aspects between *Uranus and a Taurus Moon* enhance this fixed Moon's ability to make changes, and bring a more progressive and creative outlook. The difficulty with these aspects may be in reconciling the inner conflict between the need for change and the need for stability. If other chart factors indicate a similar conflict, this aspect may be reflecting that theme. Otherwise, it was probably chosen to balance a lack of spontaneity and originality.

Hard aspects between ***Uranus and a Gemini Moon*** enhance this Moon sign's restlessness, which may be disadvantageous unless there is a need for frequent change. However, these aspects can be highly inventive and inspirational, increasing the individual's creativity and unique vision.

Hard aspects between ***Uranus and a Cancer Moon*** add uniqueness and originality to the nurturing style and emotional expression. This is true with every Uranus/Moon aspect, but especially with this Moon sign, since Cancer is the Moon's own sign. These individuals may find themselves torn between security and change; however, they need both.

Hard aspects between ***Uranus and a Leo Moon*** enhance the drive to stand out as unique and have one's way, which may overwhelm others and make maintaining a relationship difficult. These aspects are often chosen to aid the work of the life task. If this is the case, relationships will not be highlighted in the rest of the chart, since they may interfere with that goal.

Hard aspects between ***Uranus and a Virgo Moon*** add brilliance and originality to the individual's intellect, since Virgo Moons function emotionally through the intellect. These aspects also add quickness and friendliness to this otherwise cautious and reserved Moon.

Hard aspects between ***Uranus and a Libra Moon*** reflect an inner conflict between the desire for relationship and the desire for independence, if other chart factors confirm this. Otherwise, the individual probably has chosen this aspect to balance dependency, while still learning important lessons pertaining to relationships.

Hard aspects between ***Uranus and a Scorpio Moon*** are intuitive and iconoclastic. These individuals may be revolutionaries and visionaries if other chart factors support this and if the development is there. These aspects increase this Moon sign's willfulness, which may pose a problem in relationships.

Hard aspects between *Uranus and a Sagittarius Moon* are usually beneficial, though they may manifest in overblown ideas and ideals. These aspects are only a problem if the individual is undeveloped or if practicality is lacking. They are usually chosen to aid the life task, but if the individual is unrealistic and impractical, they probably indicate a negative pattern from previous lifetimes.

Hard aspects between *Uranus and a Capricorn Moon* may have been chosen to accomplish a specific goal or add a more progressive and humanitarian attitude to the Capricorn Moon. These aspects are useful for those working in areas pertaining to social reform, such as lawyers, judges, and politicians. The drawback is a possible internal conflict between conventionality and unconventionality.

Hard aspects between *Uranus and an Aquarius Moon* either enhance inventiveness and humanitarianism, or eccentricity and rebelliousness. In either case, these individuals may go about implementing their ideas or ideals in ways that are distasteful and aggravating to others. When it comes to dealing with others, they lack sensitivity and finesse.

Hard aspects between *Uranus and a Pisces Moon* increase intuition, creativity, and inspiration. However, if development and grounding are lacking, there is a risk of dissociating from reality or retreating into the spiritual realm or the realm of ideas.

Hard Aspects Between Neptune and the Moon: Hard aspects between *Neptune and an Aries Moon* are usually advantageous. They temper its self-centeredness with compassion and caring. These aspects are often found in the charts of those who fight for a cause or champion the oppressed. The drive of this Moon sign is likely to be applied to service rather than to personal goals.

Hard aspects between *Neptune and a Taurus Moon* add to the sweetness of this Moon sign. However, they may also add to its tendency to accept whatever life offers. They are usually chosen to add Piscean energy to the chart and balance the Taurus Moon's materialism and sensual-orientation. They are also useful for those whose work or life task involves creativity, for they help them manifest their creative ideas.

Hard aspects between *Neptune and a Gemini Moon* add intuition, creativity, and imagination. They are excellent for musicians and artists, as well as for those whose work or life task involves service or emotional healing. However, they increase this Moon sign's lack of focus and interfere with concentration unless other factors are available in the chart to counteract this. On the other hand, these aspects may be just what someone needs to balance rigidity or an overly rational approach from former lifetimes.

Hard aspects between *Neptune and a Cancer Moon* add to its sensitivity, intuition, and compassion. They also may add to its depression, dependence, and emotionality. So these aspects can represent either gifts or challenges.

Hard aspects between *Neptune and a Leo Moon* soften this Moon sign's self-expression and balance its egocentricity, inflexibility, and lack of sensitivity. They may also have been chosen to support a creative life task or one that requires leadership in the area of service or emotional healing.

Hard aspects between *Neptune and a Virgo Moon* are likely to have been chosen to aid a life task involving service or healing. Emotional healing may prevail over physical healing, but other chart factors will have to support this as well. These aspects increase this Moon sign's receptivity, humility, compassion, and intuition.

Hard aspects between *Neptune and a Libra Moon* increase this Moon sign's appreciation of art, music, and beauty, and support life tasks relating to these things. However, they add idealism to an already idealistic and often unrealistic Libra Moon, which may create problems in relationships. They aggravate the tendency of this Moon sign to see the beloved as God. On the other hand, these aspects may have been chosen to counteract callousness, coldness, or too much pragmatism in love relationships.

Hard aspects between *Neptune and a Scorpio Moon* increase this Moon sign's intuition and interest in the metaphysical. These aspects may have been chosen to aid the work or the life task, or simply to develop the individual's intuition and insight. In any case, these people are likely to have a depth of feeling few can match or understand. This could be a problem if other chart factors do not offer some objectivity, or if the individual is undeveloped.

Hard aspects between *Neptune and a Sagittarius Moon* are favorable for judges, lawyers, politicians, civil servants, and the like. They increase the individual's altruism and desire to serve society. They are usually chosen to aid a life task involving service to society. However, they may have been chosen to balance negative acts against society or a lack of social activism. On the other hand, they add to the impracticality and irresponsibility of this Moon sign, creating problems for those who are less developed.

Hard aspects between *Neptune and a Capricorn Moon* are similar in effect to hard aspects to a Sagittarius Moon, without the disadvantages. They enhance the individual's desire to serve society, while balancing the coolness and materialism of Capricorn, and adding intuition. This is often why these aspects are chosen.

Hard aspects between *Neptune and an Aquarius Moon* are idealistic and intuitive. These individuals, if developed, may be creative geniuses or inventors. If they are undeveloped, however, these aspects can be problematic since they foster impracticality and procrastination. The desire to escape into the spiritual realm or the realm of ideas can be strong. If these aspects were not chosen to aid the work or the life task, they may have been chosen to balance an overly rational approach to life.

Hard aspects between *Neptune and a Pisces Moon* may have been chosen to serve a life task that demands sensitivity and intuition. These individuals are often involved in nurturing or serving others, particularly the most needy and downtrodden. The challenge is that they may be escapist or unclear about their feelings. They may even deceive themselves about their motives and feelings, which can interfere with getting their needs met and developing trusting relationships.

Hard Aspects Between Pluto and the Moon: Hard aspects between *Pluto and an Aries Moon* indicate the possibility of power conflicts with others and issues around correct use of power. These individuals may try to control others to accomplish their goals. On the other hand, Pluto adds sustaining power, which helps on follow-through. As for emotional expression, these aspects encourage repression or nonexpression of feelings, which can be balancing for this Moon sign.

Hard aspects between *Pluto and a Taurus Moon* may be problematic, since they add to this Moon sign's inflexibility. These individuals need to learn to accommodate change and the needs of others, which they see as a threat to their own stability and security. On the other hand, these aspects add tremendous will and determination, which can be used for good.

Hard aspects between *Pluto and a Gemini Moon* are generally not a problem. They grant staying power and focus to this Moon sign. They also increase the Gemini Moon's psychological insight and ability to understand emotions.

Hard aspects between *Pluto and a Cancer Moon* can be difficult because they increase this Moon sign's intensely emotional and sometimes brooding nature. Cancer Moons with these aspects are likely to have their emotional security shaken, which this security-minded sign does not like. Often, the lesson is learning to let go emotionally.

Hard aspects between *Pluto and a Leo Moon* add to this Moon sign's willfulness, resistance to change, and drive for power. In some cases, power may have been abused in a former lifetime. On the other hand, these aspects may have been chosen to add personal power, drive, and determination. Whether the drive for power indicated by these aspects is used for good or for ill depends on the development of the individual.

Hard aspects between *Pluto and a Virgo Moon* have neither the positive nor the negative effects they do on other Moons. This is because Virgo and Scorpio are both alike and dissimilar in several ways, which has a canceling effect. For some, these aspects add more seriousness and staying power, while for others they add to this Moon sign's attention to detail and need for order and control. In any event, the effect is either mildly helpful or mildly hindering depending on other chart factors.

Hard aspects between *Pluto and a Libra Moon* may cause problems in relationships, since they accentuate their importance and increase this Moon sign's dependency. Because relationships are so important, these individuals may resort to manipulation. However, Libra Moons generally do not overdo this. These aspects also increase psychological insight.

Hard aspects between *Pluto and a Scorpio Moon* can either accentuate this Moon sign's determination, insight, and understanding, or its need for power and control. If this aspect represents a former pattern of rigidity, compulsion, or possessiveness, it can be particularly problematic. On the other hand, it may have been chosen to support work or a life task that relates to psychology, research, detective work, or other areas ruled by Scorpio.

Hard aspects between *Pluto and a Sagittarius Moon* increase the individual's understanding of psychology and metaphysics, or, at least, create a drive for understanding these things. Pluto adds stability and dependability to the freewheeling energy of this Moon sign and helps to discipline and focus it, allowing goals to be more easily accomplished. These individuals are driven to accomplish their goals and are often charismatic.

Hard aspects between *Pluto and a Capricorn Moon* increase the potential for compulsive behavior, perfectionism, ruthlessness, or abuse of power. They may represent a past pattern of abuse of power or a compulsion that needs to be healed. These individuals may need to learn to cooperate and moderate their drive. Their work or life task might involve governmental reform.

Hard aspects between *Pluto and an Aquarius Moon* add to this Moon sign's inflexibility, but they are excellent for research and scientific discovery. These aspects make an already inscrutable and impenetrable Aquarius Moon more so, which may cause problems in relationships.

Hard aspects between *Pluto and a Pisces Moon* increase this Moon sign's emotionality, need for others, and interest in life's mysteries. They also give intuition, insight, and metaphysical understanding. On the other hand, without other chart factors to balance it, the emotional intensity can be overwhelming and may lead to depression.

MOON SIGNS AND THE EARLY ENVIRONMENT

As we have seen, the Moon indicates our emotional style. But equally important, it indicates how we experienced our mother and our early environment, and how that affected us psychologically. Our early environment, and the type and degree of nurturing we received, are critical in shaping our psychology and establishing a sense of security and trust. In this culture and in most others, the father teaches the ways of the world and how to function in it. The mother's role is to build the foundation of security, trust, and love necessary for healthy feelings about others and ourselves. If this foundation is cracked or insufficient, we will not have the emotional resources to face our adult task of providing for our own survival and that of others.

Our family and our early environment are selected by the soul before life and can, therefore, be read in the chart. The Moon and its aspects, the ruler of the fourth house and its aspects, and the planets in the fourth house and their aspects describe our early environment. They also describe the mother and her attention to us. More accurately, they describe *our experience* of her and our early environment. Although these aspects describe both the early environment and the mother, the planets within the fourth house seem to describe the environment more than they do the mother. The houses of the fourth house ruler and the Moon describe the mother's interests and where she put her energy. If we were more influenced in our early years by our father or another caretaker, the Moon and the fourth house will describe that individual.

Moon in Aries

The early environment of this Moon sign is likely to be colored by competition and conflict. The conflict may be between the parents, the siblings, or any combination of family members. This Moon sign may also signify animosity or anger on the part of the mother toward her family or spouse, or in general. In any case, the home environment is often tense and competitive, and the individual who grows up in it may be tense and angry as well. On a more positive note, the mother may be strong, independent, assertive, and possibly athletic, and encourages these traits in her child. Some with this Moon sign have families who are involved in the military or athletics. In general, the environment is more masculine and encourages the development of masculine traits even in its female children.

Moon in Taurus

Unless the Moon is afflicted, the Taurus Moon's early environment is likely to be peaceful and stable, and to meet the child's physical needs. The home is likely to be comfortable. The family may even be well-off financially. The mother is often affectionate, dependable, and a good cook. However, little attention may be given to emotional and intellectual needs. With this Moon sign, security and material comforts often supersede emotional needs. Consequently, many with this Moon sign repress or are unaware of their feelings. Children in such families often follow the model presented them by finding comfort and satisfaction in material things rather than in people. Love becomes equated with food and gifts. As a result, their relationships may be with toys, food, or television.

Moon in Gemini

Gemini Moons are likely to be bright and intellectually inclined, and the mother fosters this. The mother usually plays an educative role and happily meets the child's intellectual needs. This is a home where education is valued, and reading and schoolwork are emphasized. However, the child's emotional and physical needs may not be attended to as enthusiastically. Although the mother may be an intellectual role model, she may be less helpful in modeling other skills, such as intimacy and managing in the world. She may not be very affectionate or emotionally demonstrative. In some cases, the mother feels more like a friend, a peer, or an aunt.

Moon in Cancer

This Moon sign is ideal for establishing a solid foundation for adulthood. Unless the Moon is afflicted, the mother probably enjoyed being mother and homemaker. She is likely to have met the child's physical and emotional needs. When our physical needs are met, we feel valued and recognized; when our emotional needs are met, we learn to value and trust our feelings. Feelings are important because they point to our needs, and only by having our needs met can we grow physically, emotionally, intellectually, and spiritually. So, recognition of our feelings is crucial in our early years. It is how self-worth is built and tantamount to being validated as an individual. The Cancer Moon's mother is someone who attends to her child's feelings and makes herself available physically and emotionally, which supports the development of self-esteem.

On the other hand, the ties with the mother can be too close. The mother identifies with her children and may be possessive, smothering, and overly protective. This may make it difficult for the child to grow up and establish an independent identity.

Moon in Leo

When it is not afflicted, the gift of this Moon sign is a firm sense of self and self-worth. Confidence can go a long way in life. This gift of confidence instilled by the mother establishes a foundation for the Leo Moon's future successes. The mother's warm, expressive nurturing style lends confidence to her child. She is likely to have showered her Leo Moon child with attention and affection, so the child comes to expect this from others. This may, in part, be a self-promoting act in that she views her child as an extension of her own ego, and love flows from this place of pride. Her child can do no wrong because he or she is *her* child. She is likely to encourage her child's creativity and self-expression, and may be creative herself. She is dramatic, forceful, and a show-stealer. The child learns to get her attention by doing the same.

Moon in Virgo

The early nurturing that Virgo Moons receive may be dedicated but dry. The mother is likely to be efficient, orderly, hardworking, and responsible, but emotionally inexpressive. She is educated and thorough in her approach to motherhood, studying all the latest manuals about raising children. This care and attention is noticed by the child and makes up in many ways for the mother's lack of warmth and playfulness. Nevertheless, Virgo Moons may struggle with expressing their emotions, having not had a model for this. Although they may not learn to be emotionally expressive, the dedicated care given to them is often sufficient to build their self-esteem. They, in turn, make dedicated and efficient mothers. On the other hand, the child's self-esteem might be undermined if the mother is hypercritical and fussy, as is often the case with this Moon sign. In that case, the individual is likely to become self-critical or critical of others.

Moon in Libra

When not afflicted, this Moon sign represents a beneficial home environment. The early home life is likely to be harmonious and peaceful, and the mother takes pride in providing a home that is both aesthetically pleasing and emotionally supportive. The absence of conflict and argument in the home is often apparent with Libra Moons, for they mirror this nonconfrontational style in their relationships. They are likely to have learned how to negotiate and compromise in this early atmosphere, which can later serve them well in their own family relationships and work. The mother might be artistically inclined, refined, and well-versed in social etiquette. Culture and the arts might be emphasized in the home.

Moon in Scorpio

The early environment of Scorpio Moons is often difficult and intensely emotional. Abuse or misuse of power and authority are a possibility, leaving the individual angry or repressed. The mother or another family member may be domineering, manipulative, possessive, or controlling. There is often an undercurrent of hostility and resentment in the home, and a sense of deep, dark secrets that no one is allowed to speak about. The secrets could include such things as violence, sexual abuse, addiction, criminality, psychological problems, or illegitimate children. On the other hand, the mother may have been highly attentive to the child's emotional needs and bonded deeply with him or her. This is fine for the infant, who needs this bonding, but as the child matures, it can feel overbearing and possessive. Since identification by both parent and child is so strong, Scorpio Moons often have difficulty breaking the tie with their mothers as adults. The emotional intensity of the relationship often continues over the years. This deep psychic connection between the mother and child may, in fact, originate in a former lifetime.

Moon in Sagittarius

This Moon sign often represents a less traditional nurturing experience. The mother's nurturing style is easygoing and liberal. Freedom is important to her, and this attitude is conveyed to the child by allowing him or her freedom to explore, ask questions, and investigate life. However, there may be too little responsibility expected from the child and too few rules to allow the child to develop the inner discipline necessary for adulthood, or the mother may be off having her own adventure. So although the mother may be a model of independent action and adventure, she may not be available to provide the security and stability that a child needs. She might lack responsibility and behave more like a friend than a parent. It is common for those with this Moon sign to live in a foreign country or be influenced by foreigners when they are growing up, perhaps by traveling a lot. The military family is an example of this. The family values freedom more than they do stability. They often move or travel a lot.

Moon in Capricorn

With this Moon sign, something may be lacking in the early environment. The mother may be ill and unable to care for the child, absent from the child's life, depressed, repressed emotionally, overworked, or unable to cope with the duties of motherhood. Sometimes the mother dies. Harshness is another possibility. The mother may be unloving, overbearing, strict, rigid, and restrictive, allowing little leeway for the child to act like a child or express his or her emotions. In any case, the child receives insufficient mothering. On the other hand, the early home life may be stable, secure, orderly, and attentive to responsibilities, supplying the child with the structure and discipline needed to function effectively in the world as an adult.

Moon in Aquarius

The Aquarius Moon's early home life and mother are likely to be unique or unusual in some way. The individual may grow up in a household with progressive ideas about child rearing and considerably more freedom than most children. This free and tolerant atmosphere exposes the child to ideas that other children might not encounter. However, although this is an advantage intellectually, the child may have difficulty getting his or her need for closeness met. Aquarius, although tolerant and altruistic, is not known for its emotional warmth. Young children need close emotional interactions with adults to form a solid foundation of trust and a sturdy sense of self. As a result, Aquarius Moons may learn at an early age not to expect others to meet their emotional needs. Consequently, as adults, they may have trouble addressing the emotional needs of others. When afflicted, this Moon sign may indicate a chaotic home, inconsistent nurturing, divorce, or a disrupted home life, which can leave emotional scars and affect the individual's ability to form intimate relationships later on. Several moves or changes in the early years are common. These can either cause insecurity or teach the individual to make the best of change.

Moon in Pisces

Pisces Moons may undergo some loss or hardship in relation to the mother. She may be psychologically incapable of caring for her child, mentally ill, addicted to drugs or alcohol, or neglectful. On the other hand, she may be artistic or musical. She is often religious, kind, and selfless. Religious or spiritual activities may be carried out in the home. In either case, Pisces Moons learn compassion, either through their own suffering or their mother's compassionate care. When they are cared for lovingly, they learn to care lovingly for others. If they have been neglected, however, they may grow up with the same psychological damage as their mother and be prone to drug abuse and mental illness.

OUTER PLANETS AND THE EARLY ENVIRONMENT

The planets with the greatest potential for psychological impact on the early environment are Saturn, Uranus, Neptune, and Pluto. Their influence does not always indicate difficulties or disruptions, however. The aspects will tell whether the influence is difficult or not. For example, a well-aspected Uranus in the fourth house may represent the experience of being raised in a progressive or communal household, which broadens the individual's perspective by introducing him to a variety of people and ideas. When these planets do represent a challenge, the challenge may be anywhere from mild to severe. Generally, when several of these planets are stressfully connected to the Moon or to a fourth house factor, or when one of these planets is repeatedly connected to them, the challenge will be greater. Regardless of the degree of difficulty, if a challenge is represented in the chart, it has had or will have some psychological impact.

The following sections describe the psychological impact that Saturn, Uranus, Neptune, and Pluto have on the early environment when their influence is challenging. Their less challenging meanings are not covered. Saturn, Uranus, Neptune, and Pluto can be considered a challenging influence if they are in hard aspect to the Moon, in the fourth house and stressfully aspected, or ruling it and stressfully aspected.

Saturn and the Early Environment

Saturn's influence on the early environment can be especially challenging because, more than any other planet, it may make it hard for the child's most basic needs to be met. Children's self-esteem is directly related to whether or not their needs are met because unmet needs, to the child, translate as not being important as a person. When needs are severely neglected, children may feel that they do not exist or, at the very least, that they are not valued. When this happens, their needs and feelings become repressed, and the child stops feeling. This helps the individual to cope as a child. Unfortunately, when the individual has more resources for coping as an adult, feelings are still repressed because now it happens automatically, beyond the individual's control. He or she has learned no other way of dealing with feelings. The psychological work that must be done is to reverse this repressive mechanism so that feelings can arise.

The child's needs may not have been met because of a divorce or the death of a parent; because the parents were troubled by hardship, illness, poverty, duties, or depression; or because the parents were critical or authoritarian, and emotionally unavailable. The atmosphere within the family is likely to be clouded by depression, guilt, difficulty, obligations, and burdens. By necessity, these individuals become self-sufficient at an early age and develop traits, such as self-discipline, restraint, responsibility, and a strong work ethic. However, they suffer from a lack of joy and spontaneity. As a result of their early experience, they conclude that having needs is unacceptable, and that loving and needing hurt.

As adults, these individuals have difficulty believing that anyone could love them. This, coupled with their anxiety and insecurity in relationships, could be a self-fulfilling prophecy. Because they are used to meeting their own needs and not getting their needs met by others, they are sometimes attracted to those who are cold or who don't meet their needs. They willingly support others materially and certainly have the skills for doing that, but emotionally, they are generally unresponsive. By staying detached emotionally in their relationships, they protect themselves against pain, or so they think.

The challenge represented by Saturn may be mild or severe. People with a severe deficit in early care may not recover fully in just one lifetime. Even behind the most severe difficulty there is a purpose, however. As a result of these difficulties, the individual will gain in ways that perhaps no one can understand or readily perceive.

Uranus and the Early Environment

Uranus, when related to the Moon or the fourth house in a challenging way, brings unusual conditions surrounding the home or periodic upheavals and changes in it. The home life may be chaotic or unpredictable, or the family members may be odd or unconventional. This results in the individual not having the usual kind of upbringing. It may either be unconventional, such as a single-family home or a communal family, or lack the stability and continuity considered necessary for one's early development. As a rule, children need stability and consistency to establish a sense of security, though that can still be provided amidst change and uncertainty. A sense of security develops more from consistent and trustworthy interactions with the primary caregiver than from conditions in the environment. Problems occur when the parental relationship is inconsistent, unpredictable, and unreliable, as is likely when Uranus is involved in a challenging way. In these households, the child is given too much freedom and not enough structure, routine, or discipline.

The mother or other family members are often highly independent, eccentric, unusual, or unconventional. They may be more concerned with their humanitarian or creative endeavors outside the home than with the family. In the home, there is little display of emotion except perhaps eccentric ones or erratic outbursts. Because the family places such a high value on personal freedom, the child, especially if he or she is sensitive, might feel rejected, abandoned, and alienated. This alienation could result in anti-social behavior. The child may act out, rebel, or develop problems to fulfill the family expectation of uniqueness. When these individuals get into a relationship, they end up feeling that it could change or end suddenly. On the other hand, they might be restless and fickle themselves. They feel conflicted about whether they want a home or freedom.

The lack of rules and limits often results in the individual becoming irresponsible, unpredictable, unreliable, or "flaky." What we experience as children becomes part of us psychological-ly: if we experience love, we become loving; if we experience fear, we become fearful; if we experience undependable behavior, we become undependable. So, we can look at the Moon and the fourth house and see our mother and our early environment, but we also see ourselves and our automatic, conditioned responses.

Neptune and the Early Environment

When Neptune is influencing the Moon or the fourth house in a challenging way, the early experience may be one of sacrifice or lack. The child's emotional needs are not likely to be met for one reason or another. The child is often required to make some kind of sacrifice to the mother or to the family. This may be a karmic need, in fact. The child may be called upon to sacrifice his or her identity or freedom in order to take care of the family or the mother. Often, the mother is psychologically incompetent, men-tally ill, alcoholic or drug dependent, or neglectful, or for some other reason, the mother may be illusive or gone from the scene. Sometimes the individual is brought up by adoptive or foster par-ents, or by a nanny.

The family relationships are often enmeshed and interdepen-dent. Establishing an independent identity within the family is difficult to do. The boundaries between individuals are likely to be weak and provide little privacy. Sometimes the mother and child are deeply fused, making it difficult for the child to separate and individuate. It may be that the mother expects the child to be her savior or manipulates him with guilt by playing the martyr. Consequently, as an adult, the individual believes that he or she has to fuse with others to be loved. Although the family may provide protection from the outside, it provides little preparation for dealing with the world. The atmosphere in the home is one of depression, escapism, addiction, or mental illness.

Those who have been emotionally deprived often become caretakers because they had to take over the parental role early on. As a result, they have no basis for accepting care and love from others. Their low self-esteem makes it difficult for them to feel worthy of even the smallest donation of energy or time from someone else, and the loss of control experienced by accepting something from someone else feels threatening to them. They often go through life giving too much of themselves, or giving inappropriately and being revictimized.

Pluto and the Early Environment

Pluto influencing the Moon or the fourth house in a challenging way may indicate power issues or power conflicts in the early environment, which may be due to an over-involved or controlling parent. The conflict may be between the mother and father, or between the parents and children. Powerful psychic connections may exist between the child and mother, or between family members. The family atmosphere is tense and intense, with many feelings brewing below the surface. There may be family feuds, or the mother or other family members may be full of rage and resentment. There may be incest or other family secrets that members are ashamed of. With Pluto, the potential for physical, emotional, or sexual abuse is greater than with any other planet. When abuse is the case, even what might be considered mild can be deeply damaging psychologically. The experience of domination can be very destructive to the individual and result in deep feelings of inadequacy and resentment. Later in life, these individuals gravitate toward partners who are destructive or violent because they expect relationships to be intense, dramatic, and full of upheaval.

If power struggles or abuse are not part of the early experience, some other kind of crisis may be. The damage caused by this depends on how deeply the person's nurturing is affected. If the crisis involves the death of a parent, it will, of course, have a deep effect. On the other hand, if it involves a crisis, such as a war or other calamity in the environment, or someone other than the primary caregiver, the upheaval will have less of an impact.

Opportunities for Growth

Saturn, Uranus, Neptune, and Pluto provide challenges to the early environment that develop strength, insight, and compassion. These planetary influences are positive in this sense, though undeniably painful. Nevertheless, the soul does not create experiences that we are incapable of growing from, though it is up to us to make the best of them. These challenges offer an opportunity to evolve quickly and to grow in ways that are not possible by other means. As often as these influences are chosen to balance negative patterns from past lives or teach something, they are chosen to accelerate evolution. Therefore, these difficult influences should not be judged as bad karma. Life is about growing. Whether growth is accomplished by being given the lessons we need or by choosing them, the result is the same—greater understanding and love.

CHAPTER 6

THE PSYCHO-
SPIRITUAL
APPROACH

In this chapter, the principles we've explored will be applied to interpreting the charts of three people who came to me for consultations. These charts will be analyzed by following the steps presented earlier:

1. Find the themes.

2. Find the themes within the themes.

3. Analyze the Moon's nodes and Saturn to determine which themes represent gifts and which represent challenges.

4. Analyze the twelfth house and related factors for a karmic debt.

Before doing this, I'd like to make a few points. First of all, I'd like to stress that what has been presented here is an approach. It, therefore, needs to be taken as a whole, applied, and tested. Using bits and pieces will not be effective, nor will it be a fair measure of its usefulness. Although you may not be able to apply this approach skillfully right away, you can still try it out with willing friends. Take time to study the entire approach carefully, however.

This approach provides only clues about the soul's general Plan; the specifics are up to the client. Clients should understand that their destinies are in their own hands and created mainly by their choices, and that their intuition is capable of giving them the specific guidance they need. Readings that do not empower people, but foster dependency, do a great disservice.

Most clients are capable of receiving guidance intuitively and have a good sense of what they need to be happy. In most cases, an astrologer merely confirms what they already know about themselves. Clients who don't, or who need help sorting out the specifics of their situation, may need to see a psychotherapist. A psychotherapist can help them get back in touch with their feelings and, consequently, with the energies of their chart.

Secondly, I'd like to stress the importance of using astrology as a counseling tool and not just for its own sake. Supplying vast amounts of information about astrology is not recommended. It overwhelms clients and takes up session time that could be put to better use helping them deal with their most pressing issues. Astrological consultations are most helpful when they address the individual's immediate concerns, not just provide astrological information. Besides, not everything about a chart can be covered in one session, so you might as well address what is of most interest to the client. For those who want to know the meaning of every factor in their chart, there are books and classes. Of course, using astrology as a counseling tool, as I am suggesting, takes training in counseling, which is something I believe every astrologer should have.

In keeping with this, the consultation should focus on the chart themes rather than on specific chart factors. Structuring sessions around specific chart factors (e.g., explaining the meaning of each planet in the chart) may not be very helpful, especially for someone who is confused or in pain, which is often the case. Even clients who do not seem to have an agenda for the consultation usually do. Most clients are struggling with something in their lives. The astrologer should help them discover what their agenda is and address it. Clients' transits invariably reflect their concerns, but you need to hear from them how they are experiencing those transits before you launch into an explanation of them.

When a client calls for an appointment, find out why they want a reading now and what they might want guidance about. What are their goals for the consultation? Knowing this before the consultation is useful for the astrologer, and it is useful for the client to have to articulate their goals. I also like to know their occupation and how happy they are with it. I have sometimes asked them their interests and how they would describe themselves in a few words. It's always interesting to see what people say, but, more practically, it gives the astrologer an idea of how the client is expressing his or her chart and what energies he or she is most in touch with.

Some astrologers might balk at asking their clients questions before a consultation because they think they should be able to interpret the chart without any background information. Many clients are also curious to see what astrology can tell them about themselves without the astrologer knowing anything beforehand. For years, I didn't ask clients to tell me anything about themselves because I wanted to prove that astrology works. However, now I see how much more relevant and personal the session can be with just a little background information.

Establishing a dialogue with clients is essential if any real counseling is to occur. It's important to listen to clients, ask them questions, and get feedback about how they experience the energies of their chart and their transits. At the beginning of the session, invite them to dialogue with you and to steer the consultation in directions they feel would be most fruitful for them. Also invite them to interrupt you at any point with questions or comments.

By doing this, you are encouraging them to take responsibility for getting what they want out of the session.

Something else I have found helpful is to send clients a booklet of information, which includes their chart and some general information about the signs and my approach, to prepare them for the consultation. In this booklet, I identify the main themes of the chart and ask them to read about the signs that make up their themes. This is another way of getting clients involved. Moreover, it helps the astrologer find out how the client is expressing his or her chart. The first question I ask them when we meet is if they were able to relate to the signs representing their themes and which ones they related to most.

For the three consultations that I'm using as examples, I sent each person a brief written analysis of the chart before the consultation, in addition to the usual booklet. This was a lot more work, but it gave them an opportunity to digest some of the information about their charts before we met. Those analyses are included here.

ANN

Ann was twenty-eight and working with disturbed teens and their families as a family counselor when I saw her. Her work involved educating parents and the community about the issues surrounding domestic violence.

The minor themes in Ann's chart are easily uncovered. The Sun and the South Node are in Pisces, the strongest theme. The Moon, North Node, and Pluto are in Virgo, the next strongest theme; and the Ascendant and Uranus are in Leo, the third theme.

The houses most heavily occupied are the eighth, the second, and the sixth. The second and eighth houses do not relate to the three main themes, but the sixth house supports the Virgo theme. Mars is on the cusp of the twelfth house, Pisces' house, which supports the Pisces theme.

Ann
March 1, 1961
03:12:00 PM EST
ZONE: +5:00
083W00'00"
39N58'00"

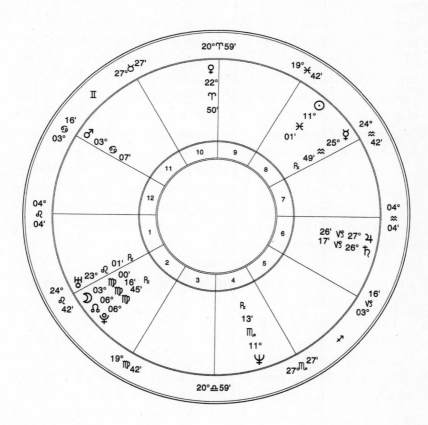

Figure 3. Ann

Jupiter, Saturn, and Venus are conjunct angles, magnifying their importance, but their signs do not support the three main themes. Numerous aspects with Neptune support the Pisces theme: Neptune belongs to a Grand Trine with the Sun and Mars, and it is square the Ascendant.

Through this same process of analysis, three subthemes become apparent: Scorpio, Aquarius, and Capricorn. The Scorpio subtheme is indicated by the Sun and Mercury in Scorpio's house, Pluto (the ruler of Scorpio) opposite the Sun and conjunct the Moon, and Neptune in Scorpio. The Aquarius subtheme is indicated by Uranus widely conjunct the Moon, opposite Mercury in Aquarius, and trine Venus, one of the angular planets. As for the Capricorn subtheme, Jupiter and Saturn are in Capricorn, Saturn (the ruler of Capricorn) is widely conjunct the Descendant, and Venus is in Capricorn's house.

The next step is to look for the themes within the themes. Pisces and Virgo imply that service is a major focus in Ann's life. With these two signs prominent and Mars in Cancer, she may be tempted to give too much of herself to others. Learning to give appropriately is a major lesson of each of these signs. The Virgo emphasis, and the Scorpio and Capricorn subthemes, give an impression of someone who is intensely dedicated and seriously inclined.

The fire signs Leo and Aries, which do not fit into the picture that has been painted so far of someone who is serious and service-minded, indicate a major inner conflict. Ann's free-spirited fiery side has vastly different needs than her relationship-oriented watery side. This inner conflict can leave her feeling never satisfied: either she is taking care of others and longing for time to herself, or she is feeling guilty about taking time for herself and wondering if others will dislike her for it.

Aries and Leo may have been chosen to offset Ann's seriousness with playfulness and high-spiritedness, and to balance the tendency to sacrifice herself. With an emphasis in Pisces and Virgo, and the North Node in Virgo, my intuitive sense was that the fire in her chart did not represent a strength as much as a balancing element. Furthermore, considering the amount of conflict in her chart, her gender, and her youth, I guessed that her fiery resources were probably not totally accessible to her or operating as a balancing element yet. I expected to discover that this was a primary conflict for her, one she was trying to resolve.

Comparing and contrasting the minor themes reveal other personality characteristics. The need for understanding is common to Virgo, Pisces, and Scorpio. Virgo seeks practical knowledge, Pisces seeks spiritual understanding, and Scorpio seeks psychological and metaphysical understanding. With this combination of signs, we can assume that seeking answers to life's questions will be a motivating force in Ann's life. With Pisces and Aquarius as themes, intuition, inspiration, and creativity may be present along with idealism and a desire to serve through social reform. Capricorn and Virgo, when combined, speak of the importance of work, and a serious and disciplined approach to it.

The analysis of the Moon's nodes and Saturn in relationship to these themes is the next step. Saturn is in Capricorn in the sixth house conjunct Jupiter in Capricorn. Whenever Jupiter and Saturn are in the same house and sign, they may represent both a gift and a challenge. The challenge may be to express the gift appropriately. In past lives, Ann may have been unbalanced in her devotion to her career, which would confirm what has been discovered in the themes. Her North Node is in Virgo, confirming that the qualities of Virgo, dedication and devotion to service, are attributes that will be further developed in this lifetime. The South Node in Pisces reiterates the possibility of losing herself in giving to others. The North Node in the second house emphasizes the need to develop her own resources rather than depend on the resources of others. The Sun conjunct the South Node in the eighth house also points to a difficulty expressing herself and retaining her identity within a relationship.

The final step is to analyze the twelfth house and related factors. Mars is in Cancer in the twelfth house, with Cancer ruling the cusp. This combination, which potentially translates into violence in a past life involving a family member, is reiterated in the conjunction of the Moon (the ruler of the twelfth house) and Pluto. Moon and Pluto conjunct the North Node indicates the possibility of current involvement with the individual to whom this aspect refers. Although Saturn is neither square nor opposed the Sun, it is square Venus. Pluto is both conjunct the Moon and opposite the Sun, indicating the likelihood that a karmic debt—either owed or due—will have significant impact on Ann's life. The past event described by Mars in Cancer in the twelfth house and the ruler of the twelfth house conjunct Pluto and widely conjunct Uranus in the second house is likely to have entailed sudden violence or death or both, involving a child, a mother, a woman, or a family member. Furthermore, the placement of Mars in her twelfth house makes her assertive energy difficult to access except to serve others.

The means by which this karma will be balanced is described by Saturn in Capricorn in the sixth house square Venus in Aries in the tenth house. This implies that the balancing of the debt is likely to occur through her work.

This aspect describes Ann's work as well. It points to a career in a service profession, possibly involving counseling around violence (Venus in Aries on the Midheaven). The ruler of the tenth house is Mars in Cancer, repeating this theme. Although this is not necessarily the only kind of work she will do, she is likely to continue to serve families, women, or children in some way. As always, the chart factors may be expressed in several ways throughout life depending on the progress of the lessons and the individual's needs.

Ann's Analysis

Your chart shows a strong theme of service to emotional healing. The Moon's nodes are in the service signs (Pisces and Virgo), as are both the Sun and the Moon. Saturn, Jupiter, and Mars are in Pisces' and Virgo's houses, reiterating this theme. The Sun and Mercury in the eighth house (ruled by Scorpio) also indicate keen psychological insight and an interest in psychology and the mysteries of life. Venus, the ruler of Libra (a sign that rules counseling and other one-to-one relationships) is in the career house, indicating the importance of one-to-one relationships in your work. Pluto conjunct your Moon reiterates the Scorpio theme (Pluto rules Scorpio), and gives you the ability to understand and transform emotions—yours as well as others. The themes in your chart overwhelmingly pertain to emotional healing, and speak of talents in this area.

An interesting feature of your chart is Mars in Cancer in your twelfth house, the house of karma. This can be descriptive of violence in a past life involving a family member. It's interesting that your work pertains to domestic violence. My sense is that you are the one who suffered from this violence, rather than the other way around, because of the level at which you are functioning in your service to others. Your compassion and ability to serve others as you do is likely to be due in part to your own suffering in the past.

Unfortunately, as you well know, when an individual has been abused by a family member, his or her self-esteem can be badly damaged. This is what I see as your biggest challenge, for although the abuse has furthered your compassion and your desire to serve in this area, the resulting sense of being martyred and unworthy may affect your ability to enjoy life and experience your lighter, more playful side.

Your Leo Ascendant and Venus in Aries were undoubtedly chosen to help bring you greater confidence, playfulness, and assertiveness. This fire is a resource for you to draw upon. It provides you with the high-spiritedness, drive, and energy you need to come out on top. It is the key to overcoming your feelings of unworthiness and martyrdom.

Although Virgo Moons are excellent for service and analyzing emotions, this Moon placement adds to your seriousness, work-orientation, perfectionism, and self-criticism. The Sun in Pisces, especially conjunct the South Node, indicates this same self-abnegation. So although your Pisces Sun is only more than willing to see the good in others, it has difficulty seeing the good in yourself. This is the basis of your psychological pain in this lifetime, and a result of the former abuse.

You have chosen this chart to balance this karmic situation. Through further service to others and emotional work to overcome your feelings of unworthiness, your self-esteem will reemerge. The North Node in Virgo in the second house shows the significance of your work in building your confidence and self-esteem. Through success in your work, your confidence and sense of self will be returned.

Ann's Session

Ann was dismayed by the analysis because she felt doomed to a life of dealing with something from the past that she would rather have behind her. This is understandable, considering how she was feeling about her life then. She would rather have had me tell her something that would have magically removed her depression. After assuring her that hers was a perfect Plan from the standpoint of her soul, we could begin to explore what she was really unhappy about. As is often the case, the issue was not that the Plan was unacceptable, but that, as it was working, it was causing some discomfort. However, it is just this discomfort that helps us leave behind old patterns that are no longer useful.

Ann was working too hard, giving too much of herself to others, and feeling depleted and unappreciated. So hearing that she came here to serve was not exactly music to her ears. It only triggered her sense of being abused and martyred in the past. She was afraid that there was no fun in store for her—only more work.

It became clear that Ann had been neglecting the side of her—her fiery side—whose purpose was to balance her serious, dedicated side. Self-sacrifice was unacceptable to her fiery side. Her Leo Ascendant wanted attention, recognition, and fun. Her Venus in Aries wanted freedom to be physically active. In talking about this, Ann was able to acknowledge that not having these fiery needs met was indeed the problem. We did some brainstorming about how these needs could be met even with a busy work schedule. This gave her permission to find ways to attend to this side of herself, whose needs she may otherwise have continued to see as selfish and unimportant.

This put the analysis in a new light and freed us to discuss the strengths her chart revealed. Before this, Ann was unable to appreciate how valuable her insight, dedication, intuition, and compassion are. All she could see was that despite them she was unhappy. Once she discovered the cause for her unhappiness, she was able to appreciate her strengths and the Plan she had chosen.

The client's issues need to be addressed tactfully, sensitive points need to be reframed positively, and the client's resources for overcoming the challenges need to be clearly identified. If it is done properly, clients should not feel upset by what you have said. However, even very positive information may trigger an unexpected response that may need to be addressed.

I don't advocate telling clients anything that doesn't serve the purpose of increasing their understanding, and past life information may not. In most cases, giving clients past life information is unnecessary and inadvisable. This information is often just useful to the astrologer in sorting out the client's current issues. I was already acquainted with Ann before I did the reading for her, and I knew she was struggling, and had struggled, with deep depression. I based my decision to write what I did on this.

MARJORIE

The next chart belongs to Marjorie, a thirty-four-year-old accountant at the time we met. It is remarkably fiery. The Ascendant and every personal planet except the Moon are in Leo in the first house. It goes without saying that Leo is the foremost theme. Aries is another theme, with the stellium in Aries' house and Mars (the ruler of Aries) conjunct the Sun by one degree. Gemini is the third theme because of the Moon's placement there. These three themes—Leo, Aries, and Gemini—paint a picture of someone who is outgoing, expressive, independent, and energetic.

Marjorie
August 13, 1955
04:11:00 AM CST
ZONE: +6:00
087W41'00"
44N05'00"

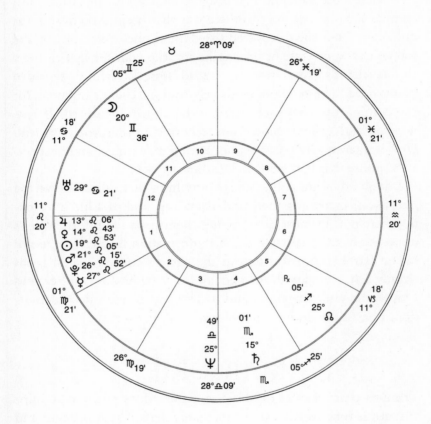

Figure 4. Marjorie

With such an emphasis in fire, especially with Jupiter and Venus conjunct her Leo Sun, you can be sure that Marjorie's personality is her greatest gift, and that she attracts others with her confidence and warmth. The Sun/Mars/Pluto/Mercury portion of the Leo stellium is charismatic, dynamic, and forceful. This stellium represents someone who has the capacity to win the affections of others as well as lead and influence them.

The Moon in Gemini does not present any conflict to the expression of the Leo energies, but supports the outgoing, expressive nature of Leo and Aries. Judging by the themes, it would seem that Marjorie has no inner conflicts. However, Saturn is square most of the planets in her Leo stellium, indicating that the expression of these energies may not be easy for her.

With such an emphasis in one element and no earth or water, we have to wonder whether this overabundance of fire is a problem for Marjorie. If the other factors in her chart are not taken into consideration, particularly the Moon's nodes and Saturn, we might expect her to be overblown, self-absorbed, insensitive, and impractical. However, she does not display the negative qualities of fire, nor does she display fiery characteristics to an obvious degree. She is practical, responsible, sensitive, and attentive to the needs of others. This is best explained by reading the analysis she received before the session.

Marjorie's Analysis

Your chart has one overwhelming theme, making its message quite clear. However, so many planets in the same location in your chart complicate the interpretation. This grouping of planets is called a stellium. The effect it has is that of blending the planetary energies involved. Some of these energies are similar to each other and reinforce the planets' positive qualities, while others are antagonistic or hard to combine. We'll discuss these energies more specifically in our session.

Your stellium is in a fire sign, Leo, and in a fire house, the first house. Your Ascendant is also Leo. The Moon's North Node happens to be in a fire sign, Sagittarius, and in a fire house as well.

The strength of the element of fire in your chart is remarkable. Please refer to the section on the elements in your booklet to understand more about the element of fire. So much fire makes for an outgoing, expressive personality.

When several planets fall in the same house, as they do in your chart, that area of life is sure to be a focus. In your case, six planets in the first house indicate the importance of developing yourself as an independent and uniquely expressive individual. You need to express yourself and act independently in a way that will allow you to unfold your talents. This is especially true with those planets being in Leo. Leos need to be leaders, to be in the limelight, and to express themselves freely and creatively. You are learning about leadership and self-expression in this lifetime. Your North Node in Sagittarius in the fifth house (Leo's house) reiterates this.

The South Node in the eleventh house indicates that you may have been too much of a follower in past lives. Your fiery chart was probably chosen to balance this. In this lifetime, with the emphasis you have in Leo in the first house, it would be impossible for you to continue to do this. It is as if your soul, recognizing this tendency, summoned the energy of the entire chart to counteract it. With the North Node in Leo's house, this is your lifetime to stand out as an individual. I'm interested in finding out whether this fits for you, and how you have experienced these energies.

You are having a very significant transit of Pluto to your Leo planets, which began over a year ago and will continue for several more years, not that you will continue to have the same degree of challenge throughout this period. The most challenging part of a transit is usually in the beginning, which you are already beyond, but clearly, this marks a significant period of transformation, both inner and outer, pertaining to who you are at a most basic level. Because the planets in Leo are the ones being transited, the issues of self-expression, independence, creativity, and individuality are highlighted. This is bound to bring up your past life issues around these things.

Pluto is the planet of transformation, and it is working to transform you. It may not be easy to face the issues that arise during this time because you are unsure of how to express your Leo energies. However, you are certain to learn how during this transit. After this transit, you will be able to express more individuality, creativity, and uniqueness in your life, which will bring you a sense of fulfillment.

Marjorie's Session

The counseling session revealed that my hypothesis about the role fire is playing in Marjorie's chart was correct. At the time we met, Marjorie didn't see herself as particularly independent or assertive, though she said that was changing. She was aware of having depended on others to guide her, particularly her father. Her father had died in the last year, leaving her with this realization. His death brought her face to face with the need to take charge of her own life and to be her own authority. She had mixed emotions about doing this. On one hand, it felt right to be at the helm of her own life. On the other hand, she was grieving the loss of her innocent dependence. She had a similar feeling about the relationship she had just left: she both mourned its passing and rejoiced in the new sense of self that was emerging. Undoubtedly, this period of transformation, which involved the birth of her fiery nature, was instigated by Pluto's transit over Marjorie's Saturn and square her Leo stellium. No one can say how she will come to express her fiery resources, but she can no longer ignore that energy in her life.

This chart illustrates the importance of understanding the chart in the context of past-life issues. Marjorie is not as attuned to fire as she is to earth and water, the elements not represented in her chart. Another tip-off is her current profession as an accountant, which is not a fiery occupation. If I had assumed that she lacked the qualities that are developed by earth and water because these elements are absent from her chart, I would have been wrong. She is evolved enough to have developed the characteristics of earth and water, and, in some cases, overdone them. Now a fiery chart is needed to balance the dependency that developed from many lifetimes with water.

DAN

Dan was a twenty-five-year-old working in a chemistry lab when we met. It might be helpful to present the analysis he received before the session prior to describing his situation further.

Dan's Analysis

Your chart has three themes: Scorpio, Sagittarius, and Virgo. If you read the section in your booklet about these signs, you will probably see yourself in each of them. Scorpio and Virgo are very different from Sagittarius. They are reserved and receptive, while Sagittarius is outgoing and expressive. This difference creates a conflict within you between self-expression and retention, and between independence and intimacy.

Your Ascendant, Venus, and Mars are in Sagittarius. This side of you is confident, friendly, and outgoing. Sagittarians are optimistic, happy-go-lucky, adventuresome, independent, freedom-loving, and future-oriented. They are explorers and seekers, always looking for answers to the big questions in life.

You also have a mysterious side to you: your Scorpio side. This side feels deeply and passionately about life, but it may not be comfortable expressing these feelings to others. Nevertheless, others sense your depth and are mystified by it. Your Moon in Virgo is next to Pluto, adding further depth and intensity to your emotions, and contributing to your emotional reserve.

With Uranus also near your Moon, you need independence and freedom in your emotional life, which may be another reason for not sharing your emotions more openly with others. This combination of the need for privacy and the need for freedom suggests that intimacy may be an issue for you.

Dan
November 10, 1963
08:15:00 AM CST
ZONE: +6:00
087W39'00"
41N52'00"

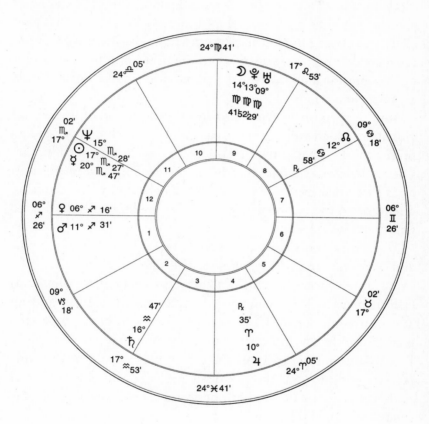

Figure 5. Dan

The North Node in the eighth house, which rules intimacy, indicates that one of your tasks is to develop yourself further in the area of personal relationships. The South Node in Capricorn in the second house points to the possibility of having invested too much of yourself in career and material accomplishments in former lifetimes to the detriment of your personal life. The North Node in Cancer also supports this, indicating that the qualities of Cancer should be further developed in this lifetime, and that your chart was chosen to lend itself to this. The qualities to be developed are compassion, sensitivity to the needs of others, attention to the emotional and personal aspects of life, and a greater focus on home and family.

Your planets in Scorpio provide the need for intimacy and closeness, which will motivate you to focus more of your energy on the things represented by Cancer. Jupiter in the fourth house, Cancer's house, reiterates this theme as well. This placement indicates that much personal growth and satisfaction will come from attending to the personal side of life: to home, family, and close emotional relationships.

Your chart shows fiery strength, with its emphasis in Sagittarius and with Jupiter in Aries, another fire sign. This indicates gifts from former lifetimes, which include entrepreneurial skills, leadership, inventiveness, courage, strength, independence, and an adventuresome spirit. These come naturally to you. These gifts were probably developed through many lifetimes with fire signs. It will be important to apply these fiery gifts to your work, while remembering to give the personal side of life its due. Life will undoubtedly present you with opportunities to develop the personal, emotional side of life, so try to be open to them.

Another area of challenge for you is represented by a lack of the element of air, and by Saturn in an air sign influencing the third house, which rules communication. Air rules the intellect. A lack of air, especially with Saturn in an air sign and in an air house, points to the likelihood of feeling somewhat insecure and unsure about your mental or communicative abilities. Virgo may aggra-vate these feelings of inadequacy because this sign tends to be self-critical and perfectionistic.

With Saturn in the third house, words may not come easily to you. You may feel that how you say things is never quite right, though your insecurity about this has probably lessened over the years. With Mercury and the Sun in Scorpio in the twelfth house, it is possible that you misused your powers of communication in a former lifetime, making it important now to learn to express your-self with caution and humility. See if this fits intuitively. I am interested in hearing what you think of this hypothesis.

Dan's Session

Although Dan had contemplated having a reading for some time, a mugging is what finally motivated him to make an appointment. Recently, he also ended a relationship and learned that his job was in jeopardy. He was looking for other employment and unsure if he would remain in the same field or the same city. He felt vul-nerable and out of control as he watched the structures in his life lose their definition.

These events corresponded to transiting Pluto conjunct his Scorpio planets and square his Saturn. This transit signaled a period of necessary reflection and introspection. Pluto was halt-ing the progress of Dan's outer life as a way of bringing him into contact with his emotions and parts of himself that need further attention in this lifetime, as noted in the analysis. Pluto's transit was forcing him to address emotional issues that had been on the back burner for some time, especially the question of his sexual identity. This is certainly a Scorpio issue and one that may have been a carry-over from a previous lifetime. The chart has some-thing to say about this.

The sign on Dan's twelfth house cusp is Scorpio. The planets within the twelfth house are Neptune, the Sun, and Mercury. The ruler of the twelfth house is Pluto, and it is in Virgo in the ninth house conjunct the Moon and Uranus and square Mars. The sense that I got from these factors was that Dan might have abused his powers of communication in a past life (Mercury in the twelfth house), perhaps as a teacher (the ruler of the twelfth house in the ninth house). As a result, he needed to appreciate the power of the word and become more discreet. With Scorpio ruling the twelfth house and its ruler (Pluto) square Mars, the abuse of power may have involved sexual matters as well. If that is the case, some residual guilt or compulsion may be fueling his sexual feelings and underlying the confusion he is experiencing. (Please don't conclude that I believe all homosexuality reflects something that needs to be healed.)

It is not important whether these two issues are linked or not, just as the specifics of the past-life incident are not important—or even knowable. It's important only that he understands that this is an excellent time to address his sexual confusion and other emotional issues that may have been swept under the rug. I suggested that psychotherapy would be helpful now, and made a referral. I also encouraged him not to focus on the crumbling structures in his life and his fears about this, and emphasized the need to understand this time as one of meaningful transition into a greater understanding of himself and his emotions.

Astrologers can reframe events in their clients' lives and give these events new meaning. Armed with understanding and a new perspective, clients are better able to face the work that needs to be done. Even though astrologers do not see their clients through stressful times like psychotherapists do, they are responsible for helping them get support from other professionals when that is needed. Astrologers should be able to recognize a client's need for support and make appropriate referrals.

CONCLUSION

The purpose of this book has been to present an approach to astrological analysis that unites the psychological and the esoteric. Many astrologers are not comfortable with the esoteric side of astrology and have focused on its psychological side, perhaps in an attempt to make it more acceptable and credible to the masses—or to themselves. There is no doubt that astrology provides us with a rich understanding of human psychology and a map of individual psychology unparalleled by any other psychological system, but its richness does not stop there. The natal chart possesses many mysteries about ourselves that we are only just beginning to tap.

Many people, even astrologers, are uncomfortable with examining spiritual beliefs; they feel they can function perfectly well without a spiritual philosophy. Seeking answers to life's mysteries can, in fact, interfere with our day-to-day tasks. Therefore, it is sometimes easier to leave the philosophizing to the philosophers and priests. However, ignoring spiritual reality does not do away with it or its influence. Understanding the relationship between spiritual and physical realities is part of why we are here, and this understanding can enrich our relationship to the "real" world and bring meaning to our lives. Spiritual reality can be ignored, but not without a loss.

Astrology gives us a glimpse of the relationship between spiritual and physical realities and grants us understanding of others and ourselves. For this, we can be deeply grateful. However, understanding is only one step along the spiritual path; the chart cannot provide the *experience* of our Self. In our spiritual search, we must eventually go beyond intellectual analysis and understanding to the experience of our Self, which is the goal of spiritual disciplines such as meditation. Meditation has the added benefit of developing the intuition we need to make the practice of astrology an art.

Astrology is a spiritual tool, but it does not develop us spiritually, as meditation and other spiritual practices do. This is an important distinction. Sometimes we mistake the tools for the goal. We see this happening in the fascination not only with astrology, but with other New Age tools such as channeling, the Tarot, and *I Ching*. For some, these tools become a way of escaping life and avoiding responsibility for our choices. They are popular because they can make us feel that we are "spiritual" or special and above the everyday struggle. They give us a sense of control over our lives without demanding that we take responsibility for them. Astrology can be such a trap.

We are not here to transcend life. The chart helps remind us of this by describing what we need to attend to. We all have issues, and we are here to deal with them. We all are challenged by life, and we are here to grow from those challenges. Astrology helps us maintain a higher perspective by showing us there is a Plan. At the same time, it demands that we be cocreators of this Plan through active participation and conscious choices. In this way, astrology is a tool that reveals the spiritual dimension while acknowledging our responsibility to remain in the world and tackle the life we have chosen.

BIBLIOGRAPHY

Alexander, Skye. *Planets in the Signs*. West Chester, PA: Whitford Press, 1988.

Arroyo, Stephen. *Astrology, Karma, and Transformation.* Sebastopol, CA: CRCS, 1978.

Greene, Liz. *Saturn: A New Look at an Old Devil.* York Beach, ME: Samuel Weiser, 1976.

Greene, Liz, and Howard Sasportas. *The Inner Planets.* York Beach, ME: Samuel Weiser, 1993.

———. *The Luminaries.* York Beach, ME: Samuel Weiser, 1992.

Hand, Robert. *Horoscope Symbols.* Rockport, MA: Para Research, 1981.

Loftus, Myrna. *A Spiritual Approach to Astrology.* Sebastopol, CA: CRCS, 1983.

Marks, Tracy. *Planetary Aspects: from Conflict to Cooperation.* Sebastopol, CA: CRCS, 1987.

———. *The Astrology of Self-Discovery.* Sebastopol, CA: CRCS, 1985.

———. *Your Secret Self: Illuminating the Mysteries of the Twelfth House.* Sebastopol, CA: CRCS, 1989.

Sakoian, Frances, and Louis Acker. *The Astrologer's Handbook*. New York: Harper & Row, 1973.

Sasportas, Howard. *The Twelve Houses*. London: The Aquarian Press, 1985.

Spiller, Jan. *Astrology for the Soul*. New York: Bantam, 1997.

Stevens, Jose, and Simon Warwick-Smith. *The Michael Handbook*. Sonoma, CA: Warwick Press, 1990.

Sullivan, Erin. *Dynasty: The Astrology of Family Dynamics*. London: Arkana, 1996.

Yarbro, Chelsea Quinn. *Messages From Michael*. New York: Berkeley Books, 1979.

REACH FOR THE MOON

Llewellyn publishes hundreds of books on your favorite subjects! To get these exciting books, including the ones on the following pages, check your local bookstore or order them directly from Llewellyn.

ORDER BY PHONE

- Call toll-free within the U.S. and Canada, 1–800–THE MOON
- In Minnesota, call (651) 291–1970
- We accept VISA, MasterCard, and American Express

ORDER BY MAIL

- Send the full price of your order (MN residents add 7% sales tax) in U.S. funds, plus postage & handling to:

  Llewellyn Worldwide
  P.O. Box 64383, Dept. K 407–3
  St. Paul, MN 55164–0383, U.S.A.

POSTAGE & HANDLING

(For the U.S., Canada, and Mexico)

- $4 for orders $15 and under
- $5 for orders over $15
- No charge for orders over $100

We ship UPS in the continental United States. We ship standard mail to P.O. boxes. Orders shipped to Alaska, Hawaii, the Virgin Islands, and Puerto Rico are sent first-class mail. Orders shipped to Canada and Mexico are sent surface mail.

International orders: Airmail—add freight equal to price of each book to the total price of order, plus $5.00 for each non-book item (audio tapes, etc.).

Surface mail—Add $1.00 per item.

Allow 2 weeks for delivery on all orders.
Postage and handling rates subject to change.

DISCOUNTS

We offer a 20% discount to group leaders or agents. You must order a minimum of 5 copies of the same book to get our special quantity price.

FREE CATALOG
Get a free copy of our color catalog, *New Worlds of Mind and Spirit.* Subscribe for just $10.00 in the United States and Canada ($30.00 overseas, airmail). Many bookstores carry *New Worlds*—ask for it!

Visit our website at www.llewellyn.com for more information.

The House Book
The Influence of the Planets in the Houses
Stephanie Camilleri

What gave Marilyn Monroe, John Lennon, John F. Kennedy, and Joan of Arc their compelling charisma—could it be that they all had planets in the Eighth House? Find out why someone with Venus in the Fifth may be a good marriage partner, and why you may want to stay away from a suitor with Uranus in the Second.

Now you can probe the inner meaning of the planets in your chart through their placement in the houses. *The House Book* provides a solid base for students of astrology, and gives advanced astrologers new ways of looking at planet placement.

The author culled the similarities of house qualities from 1,500 different charts in as intensive and as scientific a method as possible. The most important feature of this book is that each description was written from the perspective of real charts with that location, without referencing preconceived ideas from other books. In some places, the common wisdom is confirmed, but in others the results can be very surprising.

1-56718-108-2, 5 ³/₁₆ x 8, 288 pp.   **$12.95**

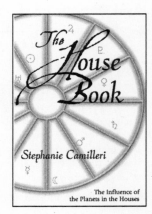

Charting Your Career
The Horoscope Reveals Your Life Purpose
Stephanie Jean Clement

Clients repeatedly ask astrologers for help with career decisions. *Charting Your Career* provides a unified, elegant, and comprehensive method for analyzing a birth chart and considering the impact of current conditions on career. You will find a fresh approach and new insights, based on the author's psychological and astrological counseling practices.

   This book will help you to define your own creativity, see the best path to career success and identify how your skills and life experience fit into the vocational picture. It will help you to understand why your present job is not satisfying, and what you can do to change that. It can help you see where you may have missed opportunities in the past and how to make the most of new ones as they arise. It even shows what kind of building is best for you to work in! Finally, you can see your larger spiritual mission in light of your work abilities.

1-56718-144-9, 7 1/2 x 9 1/8, 208 pp.   **$12.95**

To order, call 1–800–THE MOON
Prices subject to change without notice.

The Mars Venus Affair
Astrology's Sexiest Planets
Wendell Perry and Linda Perry

Are you a Playful Sensualist? Technician of Dominance? Or the Ultimate Powerhouse of Passion? Astrologers have known for centuries that the heavenly placement of Mars and Venus at the moment you are born influences your sexuality and love life. There are 144 different ways that Mars and Venus can combine with the 12 astrological Sun signs, and each one of these 144 combinations reflects distinctive sexuality traits within an individual's chart. With *The Mars Venus Affair*, you can consult the table that tells you your special combination, and then read about how you tend to act in sexual relationships and why.

In addition, each Mars/Venus combination contains a sexual biography of a famous person. Separate fact from gossip as you peek into the bedrooms of 144 great figures such as Casanova, Isadora Duncan, Grace Kelly, Keith Richards, Marilyn Monroe, and John Lennon.

1-56718-517-7, 7 1/2 x 9 1/8, 480 pp.   **$17.95**

Moon Wise
Astrology, Self-Understanding & Lunar Energies
Daniel Pharr

Why is it that people can push your buttons on some days and not others? How do you explain those days when you wake up in a bad mood for no reason? When you are wise to the changes of the Moon, you can see the forces driving your emotional ups and downs as well as your shifting energy levels. Now you can anticipate your best times to deal with emotional situations, ask for a raise, be at your most creative, or plan that romantic evening.

Moon Wise is the first book to show in detail how the Moon's monthly orbit through the twelve astrological signs influences each person, based on his or her natal Moon sign (which you can look up in the book). See, for example, how someone born with an Aries Moon will react under a Taurus Moon, a Gemini Moon, a Cancer Moon, etc.

You need no previous knowledge of the Moon or astrology to gain an immediate benefit from this book.

1-56718-521-5, 6 x 9, 288 pp.   **$12.95**

To order, call 1–800–THE MOON
Prices subject to change without notice.

Alive and Well with Neptune
Transits of Heart and Soul

Bil Tierney

This book is a fascinating look at a planet that astrology associates with emotional highs and lows. Sometimes pain and sorrow are part of this learning experience, but so is our ability to fully embrace joy and ecstasy—and passion. Our life would be colorless and dull without Neptune's magical make-overs.

This book focuses on the themes of transiting Neptune that take into account our capacity for ongoing spiritual development, our psyche's power to entrap or liberate us, and the fact that our imagination and sense of self are our two greatest resources for attaining our goals.

Much of what Neptune represents is truly not of this world. During our Neptune transits, we have opportunities to discern the real from the unreal. Often, we dismiss our inner voice that attempts to nudge us in the right direction. This book emphasizes the importance happily letting Neptune guide our inner radar systems so we can achieve a little heaven on earth in the process!

1-56718-715-3, 6 x 9, 264 pp.   **$14.95**

Alive and Well with Pluto
Transits of Power and Renewal
Bil Tierney

Pluto's path of deeper self-understanding is not an easy one, and its rewards do not come quickly. But when you learn to consciously confront this dynamic part of your psyche that otherwise remains dark and intimidating, you'll find a gold mine of psychological strengths that can help you face the world and maybe even transform it.

Learn how to better master the most complex areas of your life. Pluto's energy is intent on having us overcome our fears and self-doubts in favor of finding bolder and more passionate ways to express who we really are deep down inside. *Alive and Well with Pluto* offers new ways of looking at any personal life-dilemma you may fear is impossible to resolve—and does so in ways that will both entertain and enlighten you.

1-56718-714-5, 6 x 9, 264 pp.   **$14.95**

To order, call 1–800–THE MOON
Prices subject to change without notice.

Alive and Well with Uranus
Transits of Self-Awakening

Bil Tierney

Here is a lively look at a planet known for abruptly turning our life around 180 degrees. Commonly misunderstood and feared as a cosmic troublemaker, Uranus and its transits offer exciting times for us when our future is ready to explode with fresh new alternatives for living.

"Alive and well" is how we'll emerge after transiting Uranus has made sweeping changes in our lives, rewarding us with personal enlightenment, liberation from social indoctrination, and a greater awareness of our mind's vast potential. This book will convince you that embracing, not resisting, a future of unknown possibilities can be quite fulfilling in the long run. The detailed reports are upbeat, easy to understand, and sprinkled with humor. You'll get to look at these important life periods in very human terms.

1-56718-713-7, 6 x 9, 264 pp.   **$14.95**

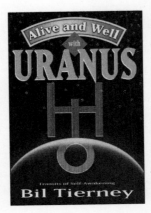

To order, call 1–800–THE MOON
Prices subject to change without notice.

Twelve Faces of Saturn
Your Guardian Angel Planet

Bil Tierney

Astrological Saturn. It's usually associated with personal limitations, material obstacles, psychological roadblocks and restriction. We observe Saturn's symbolism in our natal chart with uneasiness and anxiety, while intellectually proclaiming its higher purpose as our "wise teacher."

But now it's time to throw out the portrait of the creepy looking, scythe-wielding Saturn of centuries ago. Bil Tierney offers a refreshing new picture of a this planet as friend, not foe. Saturn is actually key to liberating us from a life handicapped by lack of clear self definition. It is indispensable to psychological maturity and material stability—it is your guardian angel planet.

Explore Saturn from the perspective of your natal sign and house. Uncover another layer of Saturnian themes at work in Saturn's aspects. Look at Saturn through each element and modality, as well as through astronomy, mythology, and metaphysics.

1-56718-711-0, 6 x 9, 360 pp.   **$16.95**

The New Way to Learn Astrology
Presenting the Noel Tyl Method
Basil Fearrington

The most celebrated astrologer of our time, Noel Tyl, has educated a generation of astrologers with his holistic and psychological approach. Now, his power-packed method is offered in this home-study course for beginners, exactly as it's taught at the Noel Tyl Study Center for Astrology and New Age Exploration in South Africa.

Students of Tyl's classroom course learn the basics of sophisticated analytical techniques in just eighty hours. With *The New Way to Learn Astrology*, you can take the same course—at your own pace—and assess your progress with the test questions provided at the end of each chapter. (Compare your answers with those of Noel Tyl himself!)

You need no previous knowledge of astrology to begin this course. You will progress from the planets and signs to aspects, parental tensions, the Sun-Moon Blend and secondary progressions. Go beyond doing mere "readings" to conducting professional "consultations," an enriching discussion with clients about their lives, using astrological symbolism as your guide.

1-56718-739-0, 7 ¹/₂ x 9 ¹/₈, 264 pp.   **$14.95**

To order, call 1–800–THE MOON
Prices subject to change without notice.

The Creative Astrologer
Effective Single-Session Counseling
Noel Tyl

The Creative Astrologer is a new point of departure for astrology: the realm of counseling effectiveness in a single-session format. For more than thirty years, renowned astrologer Noel Tyl has brought psychological methodology into astrological symbolism and analysis. Now he crowns that effort with a master-volume emphasizing the techniques of counseling as part of modern astrological practice.

Tyl offers more than 700 creative connections to guide astrologers throughout planetary and aspect symbolisms into deep analysis of the human condition. He clearly develops the art of questioning, techniques for inviting disclosure, and specific objectification therapies. Every analytical insight comes from his own long career of experience, theorization, and experimentation. Verbatim examples from his own recent client sessions are used to illustrate his techniques.

1-56718-740-4, 7 1/2 x 9 1/8, 264 pp.   **$17.95**

Synthesis & Counseling in Astrology
The Professional Manual
by Noel Tyl

One of the keys to a vital, comprehensive astrology is the art of synthesis, the capacity to take the parts of our knowledge and combine them into a coherent whole. Many times, the parts may be contradictory (the relationship between Mars and Saturn, for example), but the art of synthesis manages the unification of opposites. Now Noel Tyl presents ways astrological measurements—through creative synthesis—can be used to effectively counsel individuals. Discussion of these complex topics is grounded in concrete examples and in-depth analyses of the 122 horoscopes of celebrities, politicians, and private clients.

Tyl's objective in providing this vitally important material was to present everything he has learned and practiced over his distinguished career to provide a useful source to astrologers. He has succeeded in creating a landmark text destined to become a classic reference for professional astrologers.

1-56718-734-X, 7 x 10, 924 pp., 115 charts   **$29.95**

To order, call 1–800–THE MOON
Prices subject to change without notice.

Predicting Events with Astrology
Celeste Teal

Now anyone who understand the basics of astrology can learn how to see into the progressed chart of any individual and determine the trends and events likely to transpire at any given time. More than any other book on the market, *Predicting Events with Astrology* simplifies the techniques by demonstrating their use through factual case histories and chart delineation. In each event, the story unfolds with the technical concepts in a way that is as easy to grasp as it is entertaining.

You will come to know certain signature aspects, such as Jupiter with Neptune for wealth and squares between Pluto and Mars for accidents. You'll master the meaning of a natal conjunction of Pluto and the North Node, and what it means to have Venus as the first natal planet to rise to the transiting ascendant.

1-56718-704-8, 7 ¹/₂ x 9 ¹/₈, 288 pp.   **$14.95**

Pluto, Vol. II
The Soul's Evolution Through Relationships
Jeffrey Wolf Green

From the great mass of people on the planet we all choose certain ones with whom to be intimate. *Pluto, Vol. II* shows the evolutionary and karmic causes, reasons, and prior life background that determines whom we relate to and how.

This is the first book to explore the astrological/Pluto model that embraces the evolutionary development and progression of the Soul from life to life. It offers a unique, original paradigm that allows for a total understanding of the past life dynamics that exist between two people. You will find a precise astrological methodology to determine the prior life orientation, where the relationship left off, where the relationship picked up in this lifetime, and what the current evolutionary next step is: the specific reasons or intentions for being together again.

In addition, there are chapters devoted to Mars and Venus in the signs, Mars and Venus in relationship, Mars and Pluto in relationship, and Pluto through the Composite Houses.

1-56718-333-6, 6 x 9, 432 pp.   **$17.95**